EVERY DOG DESERVES AN ADVENTURE

PREVIOUS PAGE: Ball is life, even when it's covered in sand! Lunatic is pictured here in White Sands National Park, New Mexico.

THIS PAGE: Tanka in Aspen, Colorado.

AMAZING STORIES OF CAMPING WITH DOGS

EVERY DOG DESERVES AN ADVENTURE

CAMPING WITH DOGS

WITH L.J. TRACOSAS

EPIC INK

CONTENTS

Whisky and Echo up on top of Devil's Thumb overlooking Lake Louise at sunrise.

FOREWORD

MY NAME IS RYAN, and I'm the founder of Camping With Dogs. I have a dog named Cooper that I rescued from a shelter in Nashville, Tennessee.

When I got Cooper, he was just a few months old. He went with me everywhere. (And even if he wasn't physically with me, his dog hair definitely was!) We have loved going on hikes, long trail runs, and backpacking trips ever since, and I was thrilled to have a companion that enjoyed the same things I did.

What started in Nashville in 2015 as an Instagram account featuring photos of dogs going on adventures in the great outdoors has become so much more. The Camping With Dogs community has one thing in common: They live for something bigger than themselves. Whether it's standing in the presence of a beautiful waterfall in Oregon, coordinating a river cleanup in Arizona, or holding a sleeping dog by a campfire in the Adirondacks, these are impactful moments that leave permanent marks on our souls.

Dogs live for us, often described as the "shadow" that follows us from room to room. They're content with just being by our side. They're remarkably aware of our feelings and emotions. They don't care if it's raining or hot. They don't care if it's a short walk in a public park or an overnight camping trip. The common denominator is you. They just want to experience life with *you*.

With this community, Camping With Dogs has aimed to create a time capsule of moments that keep us smiling, a place to inspire new adventures, and, most importantly, a humbling reminder that our time with our pets is both unknown and finite, so we should all make the most of those special moments.

As you turn the pages and read the stories, I hope you'll see more than just beautiful pictures, but unforgettable moments between a human and their best friend.

OPPOSITE: Cooper and Ryan on Stone Door Trail at South Cumberland State Park in Tennessee.

INTRODUCTION

CAMPING WITH DOGS believes that every dog has a story, and our community helps to share those stories. What started as an Instagram account featuring photos of dogs going on adventures in the great outdoors grew to become a huge community of people who are passionate about spending time with their dogs in nature. Camping With Dogs receives hundreds of photos every day, and every single one shows the incredible bonds that have been created between dogs and their owners amongst this extraordinary group.

In this book you'll find a selection of those photos and stories. Arranged by season, the images here will take you on a year-round adventure through some of the most beautiful scenery in the world with some of the happiest dogs you'll ever see. Adventures happen on any terrain, and they're worldwide: You'll find images of dogs hiking in the snowy peaks of the Swiss Alps, trekking in the rainforests of

ABOVE: It's easier to walk on ice with four legs.

OPPOSITE: Sunsets are best enjoyed together.

 EVERY DOG DESERVES AN ADVENTURE

British Columbia, sniffing in the slot canyons of Arizona, and exploring many more points on the global map. And there are also plenty of images of contented pups at campsites, happily exhausted at the end of a long day of exercise and exploration, ready to snuggle up with their humans in a sleeping bag under the stars.

At the back of the book, you'll find resources for beginners and inspiration for seasoned adventurers alike. Remember: Hiking mountains and taking huge road trips can be epic, but an adventure starts with the simple decision to take a right turn where you would usually take a left.

We also asked some members of the Camping With Dogs community to share their personal stories with us, from how they met their dogs—whether it was the result of a long-pined-for addition to the family or a backyard-BBQ impulse adoption or a foster fail—to how they got started adventuring together. In some cases, puppies slotted in seamlessly to an already outdoorsy lifestyle; in others, humans and dogs began exploring together. And sometimes the humans needed a little training from their canine companions. Some of these stories are hilarious, some heartbreaking; all are heartwarming. And almost to a person, the people we talked to said that getting out in nature brought out new sides to their furry friends—after all, in wild places, dogs get to be *dogs*—and deepened their relationships with their pups.

Being a dog owner is all about love, yes, but there's also responsibility—first and foremost for the safety of your dog (see page 192 for some important safety considerations), but also for the quality of the life your dog gets to live. Camping With Dogs, our global community, and certainly the people who shared their stories for this book firmly believe that every dog deserves safety and care. Every dog deserves unconditional love. And every dog deserves an adventure.

ABOVE: Kopa models in a sunflower field in Salt Lake City, Utah, with his flower crown (he knows he looks good).

OPPOSITE: Ollie's first time playing off leash in the snow on a friend's farm in Chatham, New York. This photo was taken right before he got the zoomies and took off to play some more.

SPRING

THE BEGINNINGS OF SPRING remind us of the new adventures to be had. The world thaws, the air warms, plants blossom with new blooms—and more importantly for your dog, there are new smells to sniff. As the weather shifts from cold to cool, you can pack away thick winter gear and enjoy lazy evenings at the campsite. Hit the trail with friends, or explore as just you and your furry family.

BELOW: Harvey at the Water Canyon Trail just outside Zion National Park in Utah.

OPPOSITE: Kopa smelling the beautiful wildflowers in Idaho on a hike.

HARVEY & JENNIE

An occupational therapist learns that her service dog is her everything dog.

In February 2018, I was on medical leave and had a couple of weeks off work where I wasn't allowed to do much physical activity. I'd always wanted a puppy, and I thought, What better time to get one than when you have to stay at home? So I found Harvey, then drove eight hours to get him. He was about twelve weeks old at the time. I was able to be with him 24/7 for his first two weeks with me, and I think that really helped our bond.

I knew from the beginning that I wanted him to be a therapy dog. I'm an occupational therapist by trade, so I knew that was what I wanted to train him to do. But at the outset I did not fully expect that he would become my perfect dog and that I could take him on all my adventures.

Harvey is a giant clumsy goofball. He loves physical touch—he's definitely a Velcro dog! Any time someone comes over, he has to sit at their feet—he has to be touching the human. I knew he was the perfect therapy dog because he just wants all the pets.

He is *so* friendly. I always call him the welcome committee because everywhere we are, he has to greet everyone. He just loves people, dogs—everything. I learned as his

ABOVE: Hiking a trail in Sycamore Canyon Open Space Preserve in San Diego County, California. Harvey carries his own backpack filled with water and treats!

OPPOSITE: Harvey during a camping weekend in Big Sur, spending time at Pfeiffer Beach. Right behind Harvey is the iconic keyhole arch. (Fun fact, Jennie's hometown is Monterey, California, neighboring city to Big Sur.)

Honestly, it's Harvey's world, and I'm kind of just living in it.

handler that I have to interact with a lot of people because *he* wants to interact with a lot of people. I think he's more outgoing than I thought I could ever be.

Honestly, it's Harvey's world, and I'm kind of just living in it.

When I got Harvey, I already loved traveling and loved hiking; I'd started backpacking a year or two earlier. Our first hike was when he was about six months. It was very easy, not long, and we built up from there. We were hiking about once a month together at the time, which we then increased.

When Harvey started hiking with me, he was all about it, wagging his tail and smiling. He just loved everything: being out and seeing people, being in nature. If we were on a trail, he would even pull over at the overlooks to just take a moment to enjoy the view, like people do. I went from thinking he was only going to be a therapy dog to help me volunteer in the community to realizing that he would be my everything dog—my adventure dog, my road trip partner.

In 2021, we completed the 52 Hike Challenge Pet Series, where they encourage you to go out once a week and do a hike. I did fifty-two hikes with Harvey, plus more when I was traveling (I ended up doing seventy hikes myself). Harvey absolutely loves backpacking. He'll hike all day, then he'll take off his pack

LEFT: One of Harvey and Jennie's favorite San Diego County hikes: Corte Madera Trail in Cleveland National Forest.

OPPOSITE: Harvey at Third Lake in Big Pine, California.

LEFT: Walking up to Lake Three views in Big Pine, Harvey and Jennie enjoyed breakfast with front-row lake views.

OPPOSITE: Harvey and Jennie's favorite area to explore different trails: Mount Laguna, California, only an hour away from the city of San Diego. Here, Harvey is hiking the Big Laguna Mountain Loop Trail.

when we get to camp and he'll run around and jump in the ocean or wherever we are. Our longest hike in one day was twenty-one miles. He's a total trouper.

Harvey's seen more than a lot of humans have. In August 2019, I decided to take a weeklong road trip—just us. I'd never done a solo trip like that before. So I took Harvey, I got my car, and I loaded it up with all our camping stuff. I drove up the coast of California and hit Lassen National Park, drove up through Oregon and went to Crater Lake National Park, drove through Washington and went to Mount Rainier, went across to Idaho and did the Craters of the Moon National Monument and Preserve, then went down to Yellowstone. After Yellowstone we went to Grand Teton. We hit all over.

At that time, Harvey was not a service dog, so he was only allowed on trails that permitted dogs in general, which are paved trails. Because of that, my views of the national parks were limited—we couldn't go to a lot of things. But I loved the experience of us doing that together. I never felt alone; I never felt lonely for other people. I never felt worried. I was just living in the moment, enjoying my quality time with my dog and myself. I think that's probably my favorite memory of us together so far.

BELOW: Harvey at Lake Two of Big Pine Lakes in June 2022. Harvey is carrying his food for the entire backpacking trip.

OPPOSITE TOP: Exploring the views and canyons of Zion National Park in October 2021.

I've always enjoyed the outdoors. But honestly, I think having Harvey and wanting him to experience those things too has really elevated our adventuring. I don't think I would have done that road trip if it wasn't for Harvey. He made it more feasible for me; he made it a reality. I think just having this companionship with him, our relationship and our trust in each other, has allowed me to do hikes on our own.

He's helped me build my own confidence in my ability to do things independently. I'd always had those skills, but I guess I never really trusted myself to just do it. With Harvey, I think, *We can totally do this. We have everything that we need, and we're prepared.* I trust him when he's off-leash because of our relationship and all the training

that we've done together. And he trusts me to provide him with everything that he needs, that we can hike twenty miles and be okay.

Harvey's going through a transition from being a therapy dog to a service dog because of some medical things that I'm going through. Now he's morphing into literally the perfect companion, because he will be helping me with my mobility during a year of surgeries and recovery.

Our lives will be so different. We won't be adventuring as much as we would like to. With the limited mobility that I'm going to have after my surgeries, I definitely won't be at the capacity of adventuring as I was this year or in previous years. My goal for us, for him and for me, is to just get back out there—wherever and however that looks. Even if it's just once, my goal is to find a way back to our adventures.

—@helperharvey

Near Harvey and Jennie's campsite just outside Zion National Park in 2021. Harvey is wearing a cooling scarf to help with the hot temperatures of Utah.

LENYA & MIKE

The incredible adventures of an introvert and a supermutt.

It was 2011 and I had just moved to upstate New York for a new job. I've always been kind of introverted—I don't like big groups, don't go to bars—and I was a little lonely. So I started looking for a dog. I searched on *Petfinder* for a few months. I was always looking for a Doberman mix—I really like how they look, and how they're very loyal companions.

I looked through a bunch of dogs and saw Lenya's photo. Basically, I was immediately in love because she's absolutely adorable. She's eleven now and she still looks like a puppy. But when she was four months old, she was just so adorable.

She was in a kill shelter in West Virginia. So immediately I reached out to the shelter people and we met at some McDonald's in Danbury, Connecticut, to do the handoff.

I gave them cash, they handed me the dog. Since then, it's just been Lenya and me.

Lenya was in pretty bad shape when I got her. She couldn't even go up and down stairs. She was scared of everything. Still, to this day, she's afraid of dumpsters and I don't know why. Guns, knives—I don't know how she understands what they are, but she doesn't like

ABOVE: Mike's partner in crime and sidekick always. Enjoying the beautiful scenery in Big Pine Lakes, California.

OPPOSITE: Lenya says "It's dinnertime!" in Desolation Wilderness, California.

Everywhere she goes, she's loved.

that type of stuff. I don't know what she went through before she came to me.

With my job then I had a lot of free time, and I spent two, three, four hours a day training her myself and getting her outside.

The first thing we worked on was getting her to follow me everywhere. Now she's a certified service animal.

We were always outdoorsy, but the hiking really started in 2016, when I moved out to California for a new job. I got into a motorcycle accident there. Someone hit me on the highway. I broke my left ankle—shattered it, basically—so now I have a plate and nine screws in there. The surgeon told me I'd be using a cane for many years, and that I would never hike or do anything ankle-related ever again. For me, that was motivation to do the opposite. So during physical therapy, when they were telling me not to be doing hikes and things like that, I was doing hikes—real long sixteen-, twenty-, twenty-five-mile hikes with lots of elevation gain.

Now, I would say Lenya and I are both in incredible hiking shape. We've done many, many hard hikes. Recently we did a hike called Cactus to Clouds to Cactus. It's kind of like the crown jewel of Southern California for hiking: about thirty-two miles and 10,500 feet elevation gain. You start at the bottom at Palm Springs and go to the top, which is 10,800 feet. It's the same stats as basecamp to the top of Mount Everest (except for the 20,000 foot altitude!). We did Cactus to Clouds to Cactus in a day—a nineteen-hour day.

If you do that as a human, you're kind of a badass. And if you're a dog that does that, you're kind of, well, extraordinary. After that hike, I look at Lenya totally differently.

Everywhere she goes, she's loved. We go on hikes and she gets recognized by folks. They're like, "Oh, my God, that's Lenya!" She's definitely famous on Southern California trails. Not me—they only care about the dog.

Lenya is very loving. She is super excited to meet new people and dogs. Whenever she does, she's just there, wiggling her butt. But she can sense what's right and wrong when she meets a new person. She'll go up and say hi to people, but she would never get too excited with, say, an elderly person or a little kid. And with dogs, I don't have her on-leash on the trail, so I'm sure certain people who have an aggressive dog might be a little taken aback when they see us. But Lenya has a sixth sense. If she senses any aggression, she just goes the opposite direction and avoids them. With another dog, she might sense something else and she'll get on the ground and want to play—she's still got that puppy energy.

She's extraordinarily well behaved. The last time we flew, this guy reached over to me and said, "I'm technically afraid

LEFT: Lenya posing in front of one of the most beautiful views she and Mike have come across, in Banff National Park in Canada.

OPPOSITE: Escaping the smoke from the wildfires below in Desolation Wilderness.

of dogs and I didn't even realize she was there." Lenya just sleeps at my feet.

I bring her everywhere. We've hiked in Montana and Glacier National Park, grizzly country. We've been to Banff in Canada. We spent a week and a half outside the Tetons, where I was working remotely. We've been to Havasupai twice—she is known by the Havasupai People and they love her there. The Havasupai kids come up and ask me if they can hug her. We've explored more of California than, I would say, the majority of people who have lived here their whole lives.

People like to have a checklist of all the national parks they've been to, but I want to experience the *entire* park, really immersing myself in that location and learning about it. When we go somewhere, we're there to explore the crap out of that park. We've been to Death Valley, for example, probably eight or nine times, and we still haven't seen all of it.

And Lenya is always good to go. I've never, ever picked her up during a hike—ever. She's crawling through bushes, acting like a little mountain goat climbing up rocks. She's pretty amazing with her abilities. She's a better, more stable, hiker than I am.

I always say she has a better life than most people do. She's seen cooler places than most people will ever see in their lifetime.

In 2019, I noticed Lenya was slowing down on hikes a little bit. She would be really sore and limping after. Then one day, I came home from work and a piece of the couch was torn up. I realized something was really wrong, because she does *not* do that.

I brought her to the vet. They gave her three months to live. They said she had a tumor in her spleen that was becoming enlarged. You could feel this hardness on her side. I didn't even know that was going on.

She was still doing hikes. She was powering through. I broke down in my boss's

BELOW: Stopping along the road to pose for a photo in Valley of Fire State Park in Nevada.

OPPOSITE: "Did you catch my good side, Dad?" A glamour shot in Banff National Park.

Mike and Lenya always spend their birthdays in the mountains.

Lenya is definitely among a handful of dogs that have done the things that she's done.

office when I asked to leave for the day, and he told me, "Take care of your dog. They're part of the family." Lenya is like my kid.

I brought her to a specialist, a surgeon in the area, who said they would remove her spleen and do a biopsy. Six thousand dollars

later, they had removed her spleen completely and it ended up being a blood clot. Lenya was like a new dog after that. I asked them, "Is that three-month timeline still valid?"

"Lenya doesn't have an expiration date" is what they told me.

Turns out, one hundred percent, Lenya is *not* a Doberman mix. We did a dog DNA test and she's almost all herding dog, which makes sense because she's so smart and has a lot of energy. When I glissade or when I jump in the water, she tries to herd me—tries to save me.

She's just a superdog. I call her Lenya the Supermutt. What's funny is that on the DNA test there's a breed called supermutt. It's a mix of dogs—many different types of dogs combined over the years that they just can't dial down exactly what the breeds are. Lenya is thirteen percent supermutt. That just makes it official.

Lenya is definitely among a handful of dogs that have done the things that she's done. I consider myself to just be an average sort of person. Lenya is extraordinary.

—*@introvertedoutdoors*

Lenya is the Queen of 13ers and 14ers in the Eastern Sierra in California.

RILEY & MAX

A ridgeback and her owner get outside their comfort zone—and grow together.

For years, I kept bouncing from town to town, from place to place, never feeling settled enough. Then, last summer, I felt like the stars aligned and I found a place where I'm going to live for a while. I moved out of Denver to a smaller town called Conifer. I knew there'd be less social life, and I work from home, so I started thinking about getting a dog.

I grew up with dogs and I love animals. I decided to make it happen.

I'm an avid hiker, camper, and backpacker, so I started looking at online adoption sites for specific breeds that had a reputation for endurance and strength and that could handle that lifestyle. I had filters for breeds like Weimaraners, Catahoula leopard dogs, and Rhodesian ridgebacks.

I found Riley listed as a ridgeback–Weimaraner mix. Her picture immediately stopped my scrolling. I went to see her under the alleged title of a meet and greet, but I couldn't leave without her. She was very timid. She smelled my hand and then went back to sit next to her mom while her siblings pulled on my shoelaces and jumped on me. But maybe part of her charm was that she was a little hard to get. I'd also never seen

ABOVE: Riley looking out at another group of hikers on the Buck Gulch and Strawberry Jack Loop near Pine, Colorado.

OPPOSITE: On the trail up to the summit of Mount Huron, near Buena Vista, Colorado.

ABOVE: Taking a break from hiking for some chewing at Buck Gulch and Strawberry Jack Loop.

OPPOSITE BOTTOM: Riley showing off her prized stick.

OPPOSITE: A much needed snack break at Newton Park in Conifer, Colorado.

Maybe part of her charm was that she was a little hard to get.

a Rhodesian ridgeback before. Riley has a mohawk on her back all the time—I thought that was super cool.

At home, she was very timid and shy about a lot of things. If the wind blew a door and it slammed or if something dropped, she would freak out. I thought, *What am I going to do?* I wanted to be able to take her on hikes and to socialize and everything. Eventually, slowly but surely, we built up her confidence, and now we're able to go on all our adventures.

She's my best bud. It's been really cool to see her grow and come into her confidence. She's so good with other dogs and I trust her a lot off-leash. I definitely feel blessed. Different dogs have such different DNA, behavioral tendencies, breed instincts, and things like that. And so far, I think I won the lottery.

Recently, we went on a backpacking trip in Utah. We hiked the Uinta Highline, a one-hundred-mile trail through the Uinta Mountains, just east of Salt Lake City. We started with a friend, but unfortunately he injured his knee pretty early on and had to bail out. After saying goodbye, Riley and I kept on hiking.

I was feeling really down and emotional and wondering if we should quit, but we pushed on a couple more miles before the sun started to set. We had to rush to set up camp and get into the tent because the mosquitoes were really coming in, but I could tell that we'd gotten to a good spot and it would be super pretty.

The previous couple of days had been rainy and wet, but the next morning I opened the tent and the sun was shining on a snowcapped mountain and a lake was reflecting everything—and my dog was just prancing through a field

chasing a butterfly. Then she came back into the tent, sat on the sleeping bag next to me, and put her head in my lap. I just thought, *This is where we belong. We're in the right place.*

We finished the rest of the thirty-six miles in the next couple of days. I was so incredibly proud of us, and her especially.

Something I think about a lot on these multi-day trips is that Riley doesn't know if we're ever going back home. Maybe she thinks, *Oh, this is our life now.* She's totally trusting me. That's something I don't take lightly. The fact that she hiked with me through rain and marshes and

Riley checking out the other dogs walking around at Beaver Ranch Park in Conifer, Colorado.

It's not lost on me that I'm connected with this animal in a deep, meaningful way.

mosquitoes—it underscores our bond and our trust. It's not lost on me that I'm connected with this animal in a deep, meaningful way.

I feel like a dog is a mirror. When we're negotiating with our dog for them to push past their edge and get a little uncomfortable in order to then have access to beauty and activities and a social life and all those things, we learn lessons about what holds us back. Humans have to navigate all that as well.

There's your comfort zone, there's a growth zone, and there's the danger zone—we don't want to go there. For Riley and me, it was about finding that edge, the place where we're nervous but not going too far, and then using incentives and rewards to safely push a little bit further. Then, we grow.

It's a different world out in nature. For the dog, there's just so much more stimuli and smells and animals and people and distractions. It can be frustrating when your dog walks so nicely next to you when you're walking around the block, and then you go on a hike and they're pulling like crazy. My advice would be to take it slow and focus on training. Because when you go slowly, you kind of prevent the bad habits from forming. I know that we all want to be running through the fields with our super-obedient dogs off-leash, but it takes a long time. In fact, the journey never ends! So take it slow and be patient with your dog and with yourself.

The relationship that you can build while hiking and camping with your dog is super special. And even though it does take a lot of work to be able to go out there, and you feel so hypervigilant, worrying what your dog is going to do, once the light bulb goes off—for both you and your dog—there's nothing better.

When you're camping, backpacking, or hiking, you encounter all of these challenges and obstacles along the way—and I think that's exponentially so when you do it all with a dog. The mindset that has really helped me, and that maybe others can explore, is looking at it almost like a game: looking forward to the obstacle, laughing at yourself when your dog tracks mud into your tent or rips a hole in your sleeping bag. It's kind of a dance.

I think we put so much pressure on ourselves to get it right the first time. And what's nice about a hike or camp or a long-distance backpacking trip is that it's a series of moments. We hear all these clichés, like: "A journey of one thousand miles begins with one step." When you're hiking or trying to get to that campsite or mountaintop, you're literally getting there one step at a time.

I'm very aware that we're asking our dogs to do a lot of undogly things—things that are just not natural to a dog—so it takes a lot of time and effort. But every time you go out with your dog and put in the work, you both level up. As you chip away at that, eventually it becomes a smooth and seamless process. Not being so hard on ourselves really serves to get us into a place of growth, exploration, and adventure.

—*@goaheadriley* and *@maxontrack*

Taking a nap on Anderson Pass at 12,700 feet on the Uinta Highline Trail near Salt Lake City, Utah.

JD, WINTER, JASMINE & CHRIS

Two Korean dogs find each other and their forever family across the Pacific Ocean.

Jasmine is from Korea, and when we decided we were ready for a dog in late 2019, we found a few adoption organizations that try to place dogs from there in other countries. We were looking through all the photos on the Free Korean Dogs website and found JD. He stuck out to us—his personality really came through in the photos and videos we saw.

So we started the adoption process. We were impressed by the level of vetting they did; someone actually came over to visit our place to make sure it was suitable.

Once we were approved, Free Korean Dogs told us what flight JD would be on. They have a flight volunteer who is connected to the dogs on the flight and sees them through quarantine and customs. So JD flew into Vancouver, and we were waiting in the arrivals area—just like you'd wait for someone coming to visit you. Two or three other dogs traveled with him, so there were other folks waiting too who we connected with while we were there. It was quite emotional when JD came. He was in a crate, and he'd been on a nine-hour-plus flight and was clearly wondering what was going on.

When we got him home, JD was quite nervous. He quickly wedged himself under

ABOVE: Set up for the night in the shadow of the Rockies in Banff, Alberta.

OPPOSITE: Winter and JD enjoying a sunny hike up Parker Ridge Trail in the Rockies.

ABOVE: JD greets a new day from the rooftop tent at Kalamalka Lake, British Columbia.

OPPOSITE: Winter gets cozy in the back of the vehicle on a fall day at Porteau Cove, British Columbia.

a couch. When we lifted it up, he found another corner to hide in. Slowly but surely, though, he came out of his shell.

We weren't planning to get another dog for about two years. But, about a year after JD arrived, Jasmine saw a picture of a dog on the Instagram account of a Korean shelter called Help Shelter. The dog didn't even have a name, just a number. She looked so timid and afraid in her photos and videos. The shelter said she would take food but she wouldn't let anybody touch her.

We both immediately felt a connection with this dog. But JD was still finding his way, and we were a little bit worried about first-dog syndrome with him—that if a new dog just showed up, he'd think, *Wait, what's going on?*

But we kept thinking about this dog, and the shelter kept posting about her because she hadn't had any real adoption interest. So we decided we had the space, we put in our application, and we were approved.

Going from zero dogs to one dog was a bigger transition than going from one to two

because we knew the routine and we had a setup in place.

Once she arrived, Winter took a bit longer to decompress than JD. She was comfortable in her crate, so we let her be in there. She would venture out a little bit and then just go back in.

Then JD started sniffing around. He seemed interested. We don't know if JD started doing it first or if we did, but we started hanging out near Winter's crate. She would sit in there with her back turned to us. But JD would come and play around with us in front of her. It seemed like he was kind of showing her, "Hey, look. No need to worry. It's all good here." At one point he hopped in and just sat next to her in the crate, but he faced us while Winter had her back to us.

We think dogs are pretty sensitive to each other. JD could tell what a permanent fixture

Winter and JD take a break on some tidal rocks before their next swim on Savary Island, British Columbia.

Winter was going to be, but also that she was taking time to get comfortable. Little by little, she came out of her shell. JD helped us out a lot with that process.

We started getting more into camping in February 2020, before we got Winter. We rented a camper van and went to Porteau Cove, a campsite not far outside Vancouver, for the weekend. It was really cool, and JD seemed to take to being out in nature and walking along the big rocky beach. In the summer, we went camping a couple of times around Vancouver. We had a little hatchback, and we'd pack up JD's crate and our tents and all this stuff—we'd cram it all in and go camping. That's when we really got the bug for getting outdoors.

In 2021, we set a goal to go camping every month of the year. We rented a van in January, to be a little warmer, and that was Winter's introduction to camping. The sleeping arrangements were a bit cozy, and there were noises outside, and it was windy and cold. Winter had just gotten settled in at the house, so she was probably thinking, *I thought we had a comfortable home we lived in? What the heck is this?* But she did okay. JD was a little bit more of an experienced camping dog, so he showed her the way. Eventually, she settled into it and seemed to think it was pretty cool.

Little by little, she came out of her shell. JD helped us out a lot with that process.

Around that time we upgraded our vehicle—it just didn't fit two dogs and all our gear. In the winter, we'd go tent camping in places that had power so we could plug in a heater. In the spring, we went anywhere as we didn't need to have power with the warmer weather. In the summer, we stayed at sites that were all right next to water. Every time we go, it's kind of like problem solving: You think, *How can we make this a little more comfortable for ourselves and the dogs?*

We had camped at least once, and sometimes twice, each month through the first eleven months of 2021. But then December was looking pretty touch and go. We had a

JD admiring the beautiful scenery of Chilliwack Lake, British Columbia.

spot lined up, but there was a big snow dump on the way. We decided to just go do it. We got covered in snow overnight but got to enjoy a bit of a winter wonderland the next day, being out in nature with a fresh layer of snow all around us. And we accomplished our goal of camping in every month of the year.

By this time we had moved away from the ground tent. We built a platform in the car so with the seats down we had enough room to all sleep in the back together. We could get into this one position where everybody was not lying on top of somebody, with the dogs sleeping right between our legs for us to fit—but then one of them always decided they wanted to move or roll over. So it was cozy, but not the most comfortable. For the next upgrade to our camping setup, we got a rooftop tent for our vehicle.

We spent two weeks in the Rockies during September in our new rooftop tent and it was a really magical experience. We also recently went out to Tofino for a long weekend and camped right near the beach. A perfect spot for both dogs and humans. Earlier in the summer we took a camping trip to south Vancouver Island and Savary Island on the Sunshine Coast.

This has become kind of a lifestyle now. That seems to be where the disposable income goes—we're always thinking, *What sort of upgrade do we need to make all of us more comfortable and the experience more enjoyable?*

We've connected with other people online who have adopted dogs, including from shelters in Korea. Often they'll say something like, "We got our dog a week ago and he or she's still just sitting there, not really engaging." We just try to encourage people and let them know it does take time. Winter's been here almost two years, but even still we'll notice things that show she's just now getting a little more comfortable doing something. Every day they get a little bit more comfortable. It takes time—I think that's the key thing to remember.

The camping, adventuring, and that sort of stuff—our interests are really aligned with JD's and Winter's. Outdoors is where Winter gets supercharged. Even at home these days,

she's still a bit shy from time to time. She's very loving and comfortable and happy, but cautious sometimes. But then if we go out in the forest where they can go off-leash, she's just like a bat out of hell.

When they're out in their element tearing around, we always think about Winter, when we first saw her and were waiting for her to come to us. It was a hard wait because we were attached to her and she was our dog, but we knew she was still sleeping in this metal cage, not knowing what was going on. Thinking back to that and watching what her life is like now and how much she totally embraces it—it's a really touching, poignant thing to see.

—*@roaming.we.go*

ABOVE: JD and Winter enjoying some shade next to the Jeep at Twenty Mile Bay Recreation Site on Harrison Lake, British Columbia.

OPPOSITE: Family photo in front of the iconic Emerald Lake Lodge in Yoho National Park, British Columbia.

KOPA & KENZIE

Nature brings out the confidence in a therapy dog.

I've wanted a dog pretty much my entire life, and I was just waiting around for the appropriate time and place to get one. During the pandemic, I ended up having to put my education and a lot of other things on hold, so I thought, Now seems like a great time to look for a dog.

I have allergies to nature and animals, which is an unfortunate combination. I wish I didn't have to be so particular, because I would have loved to rescue a dog and I hope someday to be able to do that. So I needed a dog who was hypoallergenic, and I wanted one that I could take on hikes, backpacking, and camping. And then I wanted a dog that had a good temperament and that I could train to be a therapy dog, because I'm a mental health therapist.

I ended up going through a local breeder who did a good job raising her dogs. I put down a deposit on Kopa a month after the pandemic started, and I was in full-fledged puppy time for lockdown.

When Kopa was about seven or eight weeks old, I brought him home. That weekend, we went out for our first hike. He only weighed about six pounds and I carried him in a backpack for most of it. I'd let him out every now and again, and he

ABOVE: Sunbathing during a summer hike in Provo Canyon, Utah.

OPPOSITE: Enjoying the pink colors at Capitol Hill during cherry blossom season in Salt Lake City, Utah.

When he's out on the trail, he's one hundred percent in his zone. That's where he belongs.

had that little puppy thing where he just wanted to follow me everywhere. It was so fun. I'm so grateful for my friend who went with us and took videos and a ton of pictures, because looking back at it now, it's just so precious.

I think Kopa had a hard time stepping into his personality because he was the runt of the litter. He had six or seven siblings, and the biggest puppy was twice his size—a significant difference. As a puppy, he was often stepped over.

He's struggled with confidence, but not when we're hiking. Hiking is the one area where, if he's outside, if he's on a trail, he is alpha. He owns it. He has to be in front. He will heel to whatever human is in front—I may have the treats, but if one of my friends or family is walking in front of me, he will heel to them because they're at the head of the

BELOW: Soaking in the beautiful, golden, autumn colors of the Aspen trees in Millcreek Canyon in Salt Lake City. There are only about two weeks of peak color, so Kopa and Kenzie had to wait nearly an hour for parking!

OPPOSITE: Kopa and Kenzie out on a winter hike in Malan's Peak in Ogden, Utah.

pack. And he has to be in front of all other dogs. At home, he gets startled by the moving fan, by a laundry basket, by dumb stuff. But when he's out on the trail, he's one hundred percent in his zone. That's where he belongs.

Kopa just got certified officially as a therapy dog. He turned two in April 2022, and I've been working with him pretty much since I got him. I did a lot of the training myself, because of the pandemic and limited resources available during that time.

His first year, we lived in Denver, where I was getting an animal-assisted social work certificate with my master's degree. We also did at-home basic training and worked on socializing. We got his AKC Canine Good Citizen certification, and he got certified as a therapy animal through Pet Partners, which is a nationally ranked organization. I also got approved through the company I work for because they've never allowed a therapy dog before. I created this whole program that basically says I can bring my dog to work (and here are all of his qualifications. . .).

In the office with me, Kopa caught on really quickly that we can play when no one is around, but when a patient comes in, it's time to settle down. He's really good at telling people who are meh about dogs from people who love dogs. If someone isn't a dog person, he'll sit in his bed away from them.

But if they are dog people, he'll jump on the couch and snuggle and sleep on them for the whole session.

With new patients, Kopa makes for an easier icebreaker. I introduce them to Kopa, and if they have dogs, they start telling me about theirs. If they tell me they don't like dogs, I move Kopa to a different room. Either way, he starts a conversation.

During sessions, patients fidget with things because it makes facilitating words easier. When you've got a dog to pet, it's like a fidget. Petting a dog while talking can be very soothing. It gives you something to do with your hands, and it can make things easier and flow more naturally when you're in an office talking with someone about very vulnerable things. Kopa also lifts the spirits of the people in my office. Coworkers, bosses, patients, me—it's good for all of the above to have him there.

Kopa is good with whatever I want to do. He's like, *If you want to go for a twelve-hour road trip, I'm there. If you're sick and need to lie in bed for twelve hours, I'm there.* He just wants to be there for everything, and he's up for pretty much anything—even if it scares him. If he's unsure about an object and I tell him, "Go sniff it," he's willing to give it a chance. If something makes him nervous, but he sees I'm okay with it, he's willing to try.

ABOVE: Kopa focused and listening for squirrels, one of his favorite activities while on hikes!

OPPOSITE: Kopa models a flower crown for Pride at a favorite local park.

trust between the animal and the handler and depends on them being very connected.

We have the same connection on the trail when we're hiking. Squirrels are the one thing I can never win against—if he sees a squirrel, he's gone. But he knows the tone of my voice, and if I call his name, he freezes and comes back to me. He trusts me to let him know what's going on.

We love to find new places. Anytime we're in the car and we get to the mountains or into a canyon, it's like a switch: Kopa gets up and starts sniffing and looking out the window. He knows we're about to do something fun.

It's not just about the therapy animal; it's about the handler and the relationship you have too.

ABOVE: Exploring during a camping trip with friends for Labor Day weekend at Cedar Breaks National Monument.

RIGHT: In a sunflower field in Salt Lake City. (This is one of Kenzie's favorite photos she's taken of Kopa!)

That's something the Pet Partners association really emphasizes: It's not just about the therapy animal; it's about the handler and the relationship you have too. I can pick up on Kopa's stress signals, which are different from most dogs', and when he's not sure about a situation, he looks back to me for reassurance, which I give back to him. A successful therapy animal comes from the

This year, Kopa and I have been to Arizona; Chicago, Illinois; and Wisconsin. I really would love to take him back to Moab, Utah, too—it's a very dog-friendly town with a lot of dog-friendly hikes. A friend and I took Kopa there, spur of the moment, for his first birthday weekend. We tied a balloon on his back and he wore it around town and on our hikes. I think he liked it.

It's always nice to go on an adventure with a buddy who can document you *and* your dog. I love to document Kopa in photos and videos, but I don't have a lot of myself with him. But that's important too. My best friend has always been really good about taking photos of Kopa and me without me even asking. It's important to have these mementos of our good times together. Those are the things I'm going to treasure later in life.

—*@kopadoodle*

On Silver Lake Trail in Alpine, Utah. This hike is a rough drive to get to, but is one of Kopa's and Kenzie's favorites and they've done it several times.

LULU & RACHEL

A human finds her heart dog.

I didn't grow up with a dog. But I've always wanted one. So when my partner, Ethan, and I were ready for a dog, we started looking into different rescues. I saw a photo of Lulu online at Rocky Mountain Puppy Rescue, a foster-based rescue that was having an adoption event at a local Petco near Denver, Colorado. Despite a blizzard, we went to the adoption event and immediately fell in love. She was a shy little white fluffball playing in a litter of puppies that looked like golden labs and rottweiler mixes. We knew she was the one and we took her to her forever home.

From day one, Lulu has always been the most expressive dog I have ever met. She is full of personality. If she's happy, she's smiling. I'm biased, but she has the *best* smile. If she's not happy, she's giving you the saddest eyes.

She knows how to let us know when she's not having a good time and will give a loud sigh. When she's excited to see her favorite people/dogs, she'll scream out of excitement. She's like a little human and has so much personality. She brings a smile to everyone she meets.

We exposed Lulu early to adventuring and the outdoors. She has always loved exploring

ABOVE: Enjoying a beautiful summer night in the Colorado Rocky mountains.

OPPOSITE: A quick photo shoot on the side of the trail during a bike ride in Golden, Colorado.

If you asked Lulu what she wants, she would tell you she wants to be outside.

ABOVE: Ethan trying to convince Lulu that the ocean is just a really, really big lake at Cannon Beach, Oregon.

OPPOSITE: Chilling next to the campfire after paddle boarding all day at Baker Lake, Washington.

outdoors—camping, hiking, swimming, paddleboarding, playing in the snow, snowshoeing, and playing fetch. One time we even took her tubing down Steamboat River and she shared my tube. We got lucky that she loved all the activities that we enjoyed, and she is the best adventure buddy.

One big thing about owning an adventure dog is having them experience everything! Pre-exposure is a great way to set them up for success. Before our first camping trip, we set up a tent inside our house and had her sniff around it, and gave her treats to show her that the tent was somewhere safe. Her first camping trip was a breeze.

In addition to pre-exposure, we try to make exposure experiences extra fun. We took similar steps when we taught Lulu how to ride in our bike trailer. We took off the wheels and offered her treats to get into it. After she got comfortable with that, we took her in the bike trailer a few times around the block. Then we went on longer rides and made sure to stop at a ton of parks to play fetch. Initially, she was a little wary, but now she goes on twenty-mile bike rides and has the best time. It takes a lot of patience, but it's absolutely worth it!

If you asked Lulu what she wants, she would tell you she wants to be outside. She loves snow and water so much that when she sees either, she gets crazy zoomies. One time she woke us up at 4 a.m. and we thought she was

To celebrate six months post-surgery, we took a road trip starting from Colorado through Montana, Washington, Oregon, California, and Utah. We made sure that we hit all the most beautiful lakes in the US for Lulu—Flathead Lake, Lake Tahoe, and all the lakes in Washington—and our ultimate goal was to take her to see the ocean for the first time. That was our dream for her.

So, we drove three thousand miles to get her to the ocean. We thought it would be the best day of her life—and it would be this grand event that we would remember forever.

ABOVE: Enjoying the sunset views at Haystack Rock, Oregon.

RIGHT: The pillow queen on her first camping trip post-CCL surgery in Cañon City, Colorado.

feeling sick, so we let her outside. Turns out, she went outside because she could sense that it was going to snow because of the pressure change in the air. She went outside and lay there, letting the wind blow through her fur and sniffing at the air as the snow started to fall. She'll even ask to stick her head out the window during a blizzard so she can feel the cold air. She's a true snow dog.

Lulu's second love is water. We did an eighteen-day road trip this August because we missed so many adventure opportunities when she had surgery in February for a torn CCL.

And she *hated* the ocean. She gave us a look saying, "I'm not going in there. Absolutely not." She refused to step foot in the water. She just sat at the farthest edge of where the waves could reach and wouldn't go an inch closer. Ethan tried everything to convince her the ocean was cool. He'd run into the water and pretend it was *so* much fun. He tried wading into the freezing Oregon coast water for Lulu. Nothing worked. But that's our Lulu. It was different than we imagined, but watching her prance and zoom on the beach will forever be our core memory.

Lulu's relationship with her dad is beautiful. Ethan has a flexible job, and Lulu gets to go with him to work. I'll get a text during the day that he picked up lunch, and I'll get a picture of those two eating lunch, sitting side by side on a park bench. She gets to

Catching the end of a sunset in Crescent City, California.

You don't understand unconditional love until you have a dog.

PT, take her on short walks, give her massages, and make sure she had plenty of pillows. I love their relationship with each other.

The definition of a heart dog is that one incredible canine who comes around once in a lifetime and completely changes everything—that dog is your heart. You don't understand unconditional love until you have a dog. Dogs are loyal and always blindly trust you. They always forgive and never hold a grudge. There's a reason why they call a dog a man's best friend.

Lulu is my heart dog. She has brought me more happiness in the past four years than I can put into words. She has taken me on adventures and to places I never thought I would experience. She has shown me that we should live in the moment and enjoy our journey. She taught me that it's about making memories and not being afraid to look like a fool. She showed me that in life, the glass is *always* half full and never half empty. My life goal is to give her the best life possible. She really knows how to make you feel loved and brings joy to everyone she meets.

—@*capturinglulu*

ABOVE: Long summer nights call for after work hikes in the Rocky Mountain foothills.

OPPOSITE: Sunset hikes are always better with your best friend.

play at a bunch of parks, and they genuinely enjoy each other's company.

Lulu won't put her head down without some sort of a pillow. She'll use anything—your foot, a toy, etc. And Ethan always makes sure that Lulu has a pillow beneath her head. When we are camping, Ethan will give her the jacket off his back. He'll do anything for her—even swim in the freezing Oregon ocean hoping she'll have fun.

When Lulu had her surgery, she was on bed rest for eight weeks. Ethan slept on the couch the whole time and made her balanced home-cooked dinners daily to give her the best nutrients. Every day, he would help her with

OLLIE & STEPHEN

An army veteran falls in love at first sight with an unexpected pup.

I was just getting out of the military, and it was a big transition—I had joined right when I was out of high school and had been there for eight years. I was leaving my friends, the place where I'd lived for years, leaving a whole lifestyle I'd had for eight years since enlisting, and moving to Colorado. My sister is a veterinarian here, and she was adamant about me

getting a dog to help me transition to civilian life, to be my companion.

It was December; I was twenty-six and finishing up my first semester at college. My sister and I had been looking at dogs, but I made the decision to hold off on getting one until after exams, until the second semester started and my new life had more of a routine.

All of that just blew out the window when I got my sister's text messages. She had been

on her way to work and passed a pet store where a shelter company was putting puppies into a crate for adoption. My sister pointed to one and just said, "I believe I'll be taking that dog. That's my brother's dog." Here I am, thinking, *No way, I can't do this right now, I'm studying for exams.* But I looked at the pictures she sent—three photos of an eight-week-old Ollie—and said, "I'll be there in an hour." It was total love at first sight.

ABOVE: Ollie poses on a rock in Badlands National Park in South Dakota following a winter storm.

OPPOSITE: Adventuring close to home in Cheyenne Canyon in Colorado Springs, Colorado, which is a popular part of the Colorado Front Range.

He quickly became so much of my focus and my joy.

At first, Ollie was so wild that for a minute I thought, *Did I just make a mistake? Is this too much to handle?* But he quickly became so much of my focus and my joy. He helped me through school, helped me through my transition out of the military. Even in the early years, when he was a wild little puppy, he was still amazing. Now, fast-forward ten years, and the companionship and the things we've done together are just incredible.

We have the 14ers here in Colorado—fifty-plus fourteen-thousand-foot peaks. Just after I got Ollie, I hiked my first 14er with two buddies—Ollie wasn't even five months old, so he was too young to come with me. But I remember hiking it and I remember hating it. It was fourteen miles, a five-thousand-feet elevation gain. It was cold and raining, just a miserable experience. And in the middle of it, you know, I'm thinking maybe this just isn't something I'm going to do here. But before the end of that hike, I started to wonder if this was something Ollie could do.

So for the next year, we trained for that first big adventure. After he was about a year old, he started trail running with me, and he'd do seven to ten miles with me. And I did a lot of research—as a new dog owner and still now, caring for something, I intended and have always tried to make sure I did it right.

We both did a lot of work, and we built up all the experience we had in training, then we went and summitted two 14ers together—it was a duo, our first and second (my second and third) together at the same time. We've since gone on to do thirty-eight of these big fourteen-thousand-foot peaks around Colorado.

Then it became accomplishment after accomplishment—we were riding these successes of all the work that we did, spending time together and having that companionship. We made it our life.

Ollie turned ten in October 2022. He's definitely slowed down a bit compared to what he was like in his heyday, but he still has so much energy that he can hike for days.

BELOW: Ollie greets every hiker with a smile while rocking his favorite bandanna in Golden, Colorado.

OPPOSITE: Using those paws for traction as he poses on a frozen section of Blue Lakes outside of Breckenridge, Colorado.

We've lived a life together as a duo.

We're at thirty-eight 14ers, and there are two more we could do. I will eventually do them; the mountains aren't going anywhere. But for Ollie, it's transitioning out of that higher intensity. I'm starting to look at the next three, four years-plus or however long he's around, and trying to add a new hobby to my interests that also benefits him. So I'm getting into fly fishing. I feel like we can go on a little two- or three-mile hike to a lake. We can just sit there in the shade and I can fly fish for like an hour or so. That reduces the strain for Ollie, and the activity gives us a base so we're not continually walking around. Ollie is obsessed with the fish—he just doesn't get them. He doesn't want to bite them or anything. I hold them up right next to him and he sniffs them and is like, "Ugh, what is that thing?"

We've lived a life together as a duo. We have our routine. We're so comfortable with each other. He knows I'm able to provide him with everything he needs, and he gives me the companionship that I need. I think he's just so ready and willing and down because we've afforded each other these opportunities where we've been able to build up so much trust.

Fly fishing, climbing 14ers, or rock climbing isn't for everybody. But regardless of what activity you do and what fun that you end up

having, understanding your dog and spending time with them are the most important things. Really feeding off each other's energy and listening to what your dog needs will, in the long run, be best for both of you.

It's been such a good little journey. Adventuring with Ollie and Instagram took me from an exercise science path, trying to do physical therapy and nursing, to axing the whole thing and becoming a full-time photographer and videographer. Now I run my own production agency, Explore With Media. And it was all because I took a few photos of my dog.

—*@explorewithollie*

ABOVE: A true powder hound, romping and dashing through the snow at Slyvin Lake, South Dakota.

OPPOSITE: Ollie stands over a stretch of road venturing up Lookout Mountain outside of Golden.

SUMMER

BRING ON THE HEAT! 'Tis the season for road trips, so pack up the pups and your adventure gear and hit the highway. For dogs who love to splash, few things beat a summer swim or picture-perfect paddleboard in their favorite lake. While summer brings with it plenty of safety considerations—especially monitoring for signs of heatstroke and dehydration—it's also a time to get out and enjoy nature.

BELOW: Obi in Cedar Breaks in Utah, summer 2022.

OPPOSITE: Lunatic backpacking up to climb two peaks in the Eastern Sierras, California.

WHISKY, ECHO, JARED & TAFFIN

A rocky day one leads to happily ever after for two rescue dogs.

*J*ared and I had been together for about two years when we decided we needed to add a little furry friend to our family. We've always been very big into rescuing, so we were looking at a local adoption agency called the Animal Rescue Foundation, or ARF, in Calgary. That's where we saw Whisky's photo.

She had been rescued from a reserve, and she was the only black pup in her litter. All her siblings were tan. One of her ears flopped down and one was up, and we just fell in love.

Whisky has been part of our family since December 2018. After we got engaged in 2019, we decided to have a backcountry camping elopement instead of having a whole shebang, and Whisky was there for all of it. She was our little flower girl and even had a little floral collar on. It was perfect.

We always thought Whisky was a little bored as the only dog in the family—she'd play by herself and chew on her own tail. Jared was working from home and I was doing my master's online at the time, so we started to talk about getting Whisky a friend.

ABOVE: One of the Anderson pack's favorite hikes to do in Kananaskis Country in Alberta, Canada: Tent Ridge.

OPPOSITE: Whisky and Echo with their backpacking gear in a backcountry spot they like to visit annually.

Echo waiting to head down from a quiet evening backpacking in south Kananaskis.

when they rescued him he looked brown because he was covered in so many ticks. We think Echo was probably abused. He is a reactive dog, and we work with him all the time on that. He has a lot of separation anxiety issues and a lot of trust issues. We've been working a lot on opening him up. He's very comfortable with us and Whisky, and we're slowly getting him more comfortable with our families.

Echo and Whisky were inseparable from day two. On day one, though, when we picked up Echo, Whisky sat on the opposite side of the truck from him, as far away as she could get, and would only look out the window. She was so mad with us. That first day, she clearly didn't know how to feel about Echo joining our family. But by day two, they were best buds.

We always hoped that we would have dogs that would bond this well together, but the amount that they cuddle and play together and do everything together—it's just the sweetest thing ever.

Whisky and Echo hopped right into camping and hiking—there really wasn't any sort of an adjustment period. Their attitude seemed

If we got a second dog, we thought it would be fun to get a white one—then we'd have a white dog and a black dog. We looked at ARF again, and we found Echo. We thought he was so cute, with his massive bunny ears, and he was all white! We set up a meeting with him.

He was a year and a half old when he was rescued from a reserve. Apparently

to be, "If you're here, we're great. This is what we want to be doing."

Whisky was three months old when we got her. We started taking her hiking almost right away, and she would literally pull us up mountains. She just has no quit—she'll get to the end and keep going. And she's a little mountain goat; she'll climb anything.

Echo loves hiking and camping and backpacking as much as we all do. The first trip we took him on, he just snuggled in a little dog sleeping bag the whole time. We don't let them sleep on the bed anymore because they're bed hogs, so when we camp in the tent, they like to snuggle up right by our heads. It's always a treat for them.

Whisky up on Tent Ridge with the setting sun behind her.

ABOVE: Whisky curled up after she enjoyed her dinner and had a little snooze, while her humans got the fire going on a backcountry camping trip.

OPPOSITE: Jared and Echo heading down Tent Ridge with the Spray Lakes reservoir behind them, and the setting sun lighting up the mountains.

They both must have been sled dogs in a past life because they both pull. But Whisky's all go, and Echo likes taking his time—he's a little more chill. He likes to chase bugs and he stops to smell things—he gets there on his own time.

We love the mountains. The Rockies are right here—we're so close and they're super convenient to get to. And we love photography, so adding that to our family adventures has made them all the more fun.

We do a lot of camping in Alberta Parks' campgrounds with our trailer, and we do some overlanding in public land areas. We also do a lot of backcountry camping in the Kananaskis area and camping in the Ghost River Wilderness and the Waiparous area. We go back to our elopement spot every year—it was so fun to introduce Echo to that place.

But aside from that, there's not one specific spot we return to. Anywhere and everywhere is where we like to be, as long as it's outdoors.

Out in nature, it's been amazing to see just how in tune the dogs are with everything. They're always looking and smelling; if there's a squirrel, they know where it is.

This year, we've had two bear encounters—the most we've ever had in all the time we've been adventuring and hiking. Just recently, we were walking a trail where there had been some bear activity. We'd seen some scat and whatnot, and we were calling out every now and again to tell the bears where we were. Then the dogs triggered instantly. They were very vocal—it was immediately clear that something was up. It was very different than how they'd normally react if it was, say, a grouse or squirrel.

We figured they knew something that we didn't. We kept walking for about five minutes but they got more and more agitated. Then we turned a corner, and they were clearly telling us, "Hey, guys, stop." So we stopped and looked ahead, and a bear walked out of the bushes about fifty yards up. The bear glanced at us for a moment—we were calling out and had our poles up in the air—and then he turned and meandered away.

We'd never seen Whisky and Echo act like that before, and we'd never trained them to do anything like that. It was very cool to see. Now we know just how in tune they are, and that if there's a bear anywhere around us, they're going to know. We have a bear alarm.

Camping with dogs is lots of fun, but you have to be aware of leash policies. In Canada, they have to be leashed in parks, provincial parks, and national parks. When we do let them off-leash in wilderness and public land areas, we're very aware of the surroundings and make sure that we can always see them. We're also always watching for signs of heatstroke and heat exhaustion in the dogs when we're hiking in the summer. We don't do a ton of summits at midday with them when it's hot out. Same with being on scree or in snow. We're always checking their paws

BELOW: Whisky leading the way (because she always has to be first) back to the truck after spending the evening backpacking at Bertha Lake in Waterton Lakes National Park in Alberta, Canada.

OPPOSITE: Echo cooling off in the river on the way up to Bertha Lake.

to make sure that they're not blistered or scratched up. When it's super hot, we either do sunset hikes or sunrise hikes, or we hike to lakes or in places that we know will have lots of water along the trail.

Their safety is so important, and it can be hard to notice when they're having trouble. So many times, dogs just push through pain or warning signs because they just want to please their humans. For us, it's about being very aware of our dogs and their abilities and knowing the signs for when they need a break.

With safety top of mind, adventuring with dogs is fantastic—they make the experience a lot more fun. We love watching them swim in the alpine lakes, or be mountain goats and just hop up on the rocks, or go up the hike so much easier than we can. It's a lot of fun, and a lot of work—but it's worth it.

Our little rescue pups are the best pups. They go everywhere with us, and they're really good camping and hiking buddies. We're so happy that they like it as much as we do.

Whisky and Echo make our lives whole. We would be bored without them! We go for three to five walks a day with them, and then go hiking and adventuring on the weekends. We don't know what life would be like anymore without them. We're so lucky.

—*@andrsn.pck*

So many times, dogs just push through pain or warning signs because they just want to please their humans.

LUNATIC & LILLIAN

A vacation rescue brings next-level chaos—and then unparalleled love and full-time adventure.

I met Lunatic (nicknamed Luna) on a trip I took to Baja, Mexico, years ago. My ex and I were staying in an Airbnb and there was this little puppy outside, barking her head off nonstop, all day long. At first, I just kept thinking how annoying she was—and if you've heard a heeler scream-bark before, you'll understand. We went to investigate and found she

was tied up in the backyard on a heavy metal chain. There was a big tub filled with food that she would jump into to eat, and there was also a bathtub filled with water. She was too small to stand and drink over the side, so she had to leap into the tub to drink, which made it muddy.

We asked around and found out from neighbors that her owner was the owner of the Airbnb we were staying at. He lived in San Diego but had left her down in Baja as a

"guard dog"; more likely, it was because she'd started teething and her cute "puppy phase" was over. No dog is meant to be a guard dog chained up 24/7. In particular, her breed (a herding breed) would almost certainly develop severe depression and social anxiety as a result of not having any exercise. We decided to take her off her chain and take her to the beach. We adopted her into our little life for the time that we were there.

ABOVE: Smelling the sweet smells of nature in the Wind River Range, Wyoming.

OPPOSITE: Enjoying a cotton candy pink sunset at camp in the Eastern Sierras, California.

ABOVE: Camouflaging
in Red Rock Canyon,
Nevada.

RIGHT: Happy girl in the
beautiful Bonneville Salt
Flats, Utah.

OPPOSITE: Peek-a-boo!
At Peek-A-Boo Slot
Canyon, Utah.

When it was time to go back to the States, we realized we couldn't just leave her. We called the owner of the property and asked to take her off his hands. We felt we'd be doing him a favor. But he said we had to pay him $500. On principle, we didn't want to give this guy money, plus we already had a super active border collie at home and weren't ready to take on raising a wild puppy as well.

As we deliberated, Luna sat in my lap, tiny and dusty, waiting to hear her destiny.

I remember looking at her with tears in my eyes, saying, "I'm so sorry, but we can't take you." She knew what our decision was the moment I put the chain back on her neck, and she started crying, whining, pawing at me, begging me to change my mind. So really what choice did I have? I called the guy back and offered him $350, rationalizing that it was what I would have paid to rescue her from a shelter anyway. He agreed, and we drove back to the States with our new dusty little pup!

The love story temporarily ends there. There's a reason why we named her Lunatic.

She was a demon puppy. She didn't have any training and was absolutely wild. Our attempts at crate-training, like responsible dog owners, ended after she scream-barked all night long for days straight. Soon after, my ex and I broke up, so then it was just me and a Lunatic.

Her demon puppy days were long and fierce—so many phone and laptop chargers were destroyed, my door was ripped to shreds, many meals I cooked were snatched away right under my nose, and countless more victims fell to her destruction. I remember angrily deleting photos and videos of her while at work, thinking, *You are the worst puppy ever*, because I was so pissed off every time the dog walker called to tell me that Luna destroyed yet another thing. I'm not going to lie: There

I stuck with her through the highs and lows, and in the end, we learned how to understand and trust each other.

were many times I was so frustrated that I regretted ever rescuing her. But I also knew I couldn't just give up. I realized that whatever I was doing wasn't working. After doing more research, I realized that the solution to her problematic behavior was to put in the work on my end to understand her breed.

Australian cattle dog/shepherd mixes require a ton of physical and mental exercise to keep them busy and healthy. Instead of sleeping in, I would set a 6 a.m. alarm to take her to the dog park. Instead of hanging out with coworkers after work, I would take her out on hikes nearby. Instead of hanging out with friends on the weekends, I would drive seven hours to the Eastern Sierras to backpack and hike with her. Slowly but surely, her temper tantrums and destructive nature dwindled as she learned to trust me and see that I would be a good mom and adventure partner to her.

While Luna has grown up to be the best dog I could ask for, a lot of people have this stigma about rescuing dogs because "they must be traumatized and really hard to deal with!" The truth lies somewhere in between—while they can carry trauma with them, the effort you put into gaining their love makes it all worth it in the end. I stuck with her through the highs and lows, and in the end, we learned how to understand and trust each other. I can now say that she's my soulmate and the best partner I could have ever asked for.

We've been on so many adventures. But the place that we hold most dear is the Eastern Sierras. It's so beautiful, rugged and wild. We do a lot of mountain-climbing and big day hikes. Sometimes they're grueling twelve- to fourteen-hour days, but every journey, sunrise, sunset, with her trotting alongside me as my little shadow, is worth the trek.

Once, Luna and I were backpacking and we'd set up camp. We ended up having enough

ABOVE: Cooling down during a sunset swim in the Sea of Cortez at Gonzaga Bay, Baja California.

OPPOSITE: Standing proud and tall after summiting Banner Peak (seen in the background) in the Eastern Sierras.

ABOVE: Tongue's hangin' out on a hot summer day in White Sands National Park, New Mexico. (Mom only took her leash off for this photo!)

OPPOSITE: Cooling down in front of Payson Peak after a long day of backpacking in the Wind River Range.

daylight left to climb a nearby peak, but on our way down, as the sun was setting, it hit me that I forgot to set a marker for where my tent was. Everything looked different at night. We looked around for the tent for over an hour, boulder hopping, trying to retrace our steps, and frantically checking the map. Even though temperatures were quickly dropping below freezing, I was about to give up and just sleep on the ground because I was so tired.

The whole time, Luna had been following me around, looking at me questioningly from time to time. Finally, I just said, "Luna, help me. Help mommy find home. *Find home.*"

She looked at me for a minute, then she just ran off into the dark.

It's bear country, so I was worried and yelled at her to come back. After a few minutes, she ran back and looked at me, then she started wagging her tail and wriggling her butt. So I followed her and it turned out, she had found our campsite! I thought, *Wow. You smart girl. You just saved us!*

We have now been living full-time out of our truck camper for over three years. We go adventuring year-round. Luna is an all-terrain dog—she loves the water, loves the mountains, and loves the desert. In the summer and fall, we backpack and hike in California, Wyoming, Washington, Montana, and Idaho, explore slot canyons in Southern Utah, and surf in Baja. In the winter and spring, we chase snow in Utah, Colorado, Oregon, Washington, Wyoming, and Canada. My partner and I are both avalanche-certified, so now Luna can join us on backcountry skiing adventures. If you really want to tire out a cattle dog, having them chase after you in deep powder is the best way!

A lot of people see photos of Luna on her adventures and write to me, "I want to do this with my dog! But I need to train them first," or "I need to get them gear," or "I'm nervous they can't handle it." Each breed is different in what they can handle, in terms of terrain, distance, hiking duration, and level of training. And remember: Recall training is essential, especially in the wilderness. However, your dog is smarter than you think they are. Trust them to rise to the occasion. You just have to get out there and do it.

Love is conditional—except for the love you have with your dog.

Remember, anything is possible. Many people think, *If I want to hike with a dog, I need to get this breed or that breed.* Not true! I know some people who do crazy hikes with their Yorkie or Maltese. You don't need to get a dog that fits your vision of what an adventure dog should look like. Just try, little by little. Start with a one-mile hike, then a three-mile hike, and so on. The important thing is to not underestimate your dog and to not let your own hesitations and fears stop your dog from living their best life.

My now-fiancé remembers when we first met, and that one of the things I declared was, "If you want to be with me, you have to be okay with being second to my dog." And he responded, "Okay!" After all, love is conditional—except for the love you have with your dog. A dog really would do anything for you, especially after you worked so hard to earn their trust and love. It's truly like nothing else.

Lunatic's time on this earth will only be a fraction of what I have, and every day I dread my last day with her. But I promise her that while she's by my side, I'll show her the best of what this world can offer.

—*@ourlifeunleashed*

BLAZER, ROCKY, BRIDGER, CHEWY, OBI & KATHLEEN

Life is for the dogs—and their humans wouldn't have it any other way.

A common question we get is, how did you end up with this many dogs? Believe me, it wasn't planned. Before I met my wife, Tracy, I had a golden retriever named Brodie. When we met, he was about six. She fell in love with him. Tragically, there was a bad accident and he died in a horrible way. It hit us both very hard, but mostly Tracy, who felt

overwhelming guilt and went into a deep depression. She didn't get off the couch for a week. I was desperate to help her snap out of it.

About ten days after Brodie died, I contacted a woman who had a litter of white goldens. She said she just had one female left. I went after work, not really excited, because I wanted a male. But then the family who had

shown up for the male changed their minds, so she had a male. This was Blazer. I had never purchased a dog from a breeder, but that day I did. Tracy says he saved her: Blazer needed her and gave her purpose.

A year later, we thought, *Let's get Blazer a friend*. So we got Rocky. He and his littermates were in a backyard in the July

ABOVE: The dogs in the Superstition wilderness in Arizona in spring of 2022.

OPPOSITE: A photo taken on Kathleen's birthday hike, from an August 2022 trip to Fishlake National Forest in Utah.

Four of the dogs in Valley of the Gods in Utah in October 2022. The pack did a ten-day vacation, including many hikes and canyons.

Arizona heat, and I said, "I'm not leaving here without taking one of these dogs with us." He was just six weeks old. But Blazer wasted no time in being a surrogate parent.

A year later, my mom's dog died. She began talking about getting a doodle, and I had a friend whose golden and doodle had just had puppies two days before Christmas. I surprised my mom for Christmas with Bridger. A few months later, in February, my friend said she had had a puppy returned and asked if we would be interested in taking Bridger's brother. We couldn't refuse, so then there was Chewy.

The fourth dog was Kodi. Technically, he was my younger son's dog that eventually came to live with the pack because he couldn't stand to be apart from them. But Kodi had some serious genetic spinal issues, and after many vet visits, neurologists, MRIs, CTs, and treatment, he couldn't be fixed and was in horrible pain. We helped him across the rainbow bridge before he was five. It was devastating.

I think one reason why we give these dogs such a good life is because of Brodie and how he died. Tracy and I both agreed: Our life is all for the dogs. Everything is for the dogs and their happiness.

A few months after Kodi died, we started to think about fostering. The Arizona Lucky Huskies coordinator reached out to us. They were headed to a shelter in Nogales, New Mexico, that had thirteen huskies. They could only bring back three. While there, she sent me pictures and asked, "Do any of these dogs speak to you?" And there was Obi, sitting there with another dog just barking in his ear. Obi's eyes were wide and he looked so scared. I just cried when I saw his picture, and I said, "That is my dog."

He had been scheduled to be euthanized the day after they picked him up. The shelter

Our life is all for the dogs. Everything is for the dogs and their happiness.

had said he was two, but he wasn't even one year old yet. He was only about forty-five pounds. He weighs ninety now—that's how malnourished he was. He had giardia. He had cuts. He had a swollen abscess on his scrotum that they had to remove. He was used to fending for himself. My friend with Lucky Huskies told me, "He just walked across the vet's office *on his hind feet*." And I thought, *On no. What are we in for?*

This is where it became tough. We brought Obi home and Rocky said, "Nuh-uh, this

ABOVE: Blazer jumping into a pool of water while Chewy and another dog friend keep watch in Tonto National Forest below the Mogollon Rim, Arizona.

LEFT: At Mogollon Rim during the summer of 2021.

going to give this three weeks and see where we are at." And it was about two before things got a little better, and almost nine months before things really settled down. It took time and patience, but now they are a tight pack.

Obi is the most amazing hiker. It took us a long while and a lot of work to get to this point. He started hiking on a fifty-foot rainbow leash. We called it the leash of death because he would trip people up. On our first backpacking trip into the Superstitions, I let him drag the leash— he'd run between us with it flying behind him, and everyone would shout, "Here comes the leash!" But we could step on it when he got too far, and I would call him back and give him a treat. It was a lot of work, and a lot of consistency, but now he hikes off-leash.

He's not perfect—he is *so* far from perfect. If there's an elk—oh, he's going to give it a good shot. And cows are his kryptonite. He just wants to be friends with all the cows. We often fantasize that maybe he was raised with a family of cows when he was in New Mexico, and now he just always wants to check if the cow is his mother or his brother. So ninety-nine percent perfect, one percent cow chaser.

Obi is just an amazing dog. He knows when I am sad, he makes me laugh, he snuggles, and some nights we share a pillow. I love that he has had one hell of an amazing life in his three years with us.

ABOVE: Obi sleeping in a chair, exhausted after a hike. Happy, tired dogs are the best way to enjoy a quiet evening.

OPPOSITE: Rocky, Chewy, Bridger, and Obi at sunrise two days before Christmas 2022, with the Superstition Mountains in the background.

isn't going to happen." There was fighting; we had to separate them. We had a cat, too, so in addition to that we also had to get Obi used to living with a cat when he used to *eat* them. The first night Obi was with us, he slept on the couch in Tracy's lap, and he just looked exhausted—but you could see he felt safe.

Getting a rescue dog is a lot of work. They say there's the rule of threes: It takes three days for the dog to even start calming down. Then it takes three weeks for them to get used to a house and routines. And then it's a full three months before the dog actually realizes that they might be home. So we said, "We're

I don't think a lot of people understand how rewarding it can be to get a rescue. I know I didn't. Sure, getting a puppy is easier in a lot of ways. But helping Obi has been one of the most rewarding experiences I've ever had. When people see Obi, they tell me, "Wow, what a beautiful dog," and they just assume I've gotten him from some upscale breeder. And I tell them very quickly that he's a mutt. We had a DNA test: He's husky, malamute, Samoyed, German shepherd; I think there's some rottweiler and lab thrown in there. I tell them, "He's not from a breeder—he was on the list to be euthanized at a kill shelter."

Our first big adventure was backpacking in Colorado and the Ice Lakes Basin. Blazer was a couple years old then, and Rocky was maybe a little over a year. Chewy was too young, so he stayed back with my parents. It was one of the coldest backpacking trips we've ever done, but the beauty made it worth it. Blazer didn't care that the lake was ice-cold—he went swimming. People thought he was crazy. We call him a polar bear.

After that, every trip has been planned around the dogs. We spend a few weeks every year in Colorado, Utah, and New Mexico, in addition to exploring Arizona. We backpack with them, paddleboard, hike, off-road. We have been to some amazing places: Buckskin

My knowledge of the landscape has grown so much through my dogs.

Rocky, Obi, and Chewy with Beau, Kathleen's friend Andrea's dog, near Superstition Wilderness.

Gulch, Escalante, San Rafael Swell, Goblin Valley. They have hiked slot canyons, rivers, and peaks. People often say that when they come back in the next life, they want to be one of my dogs. Looking back at the life they have had, I say that is the only way it should be.

On hiking in the southwest with dogs, there are a few important safety things I focus on. One, that there's enough water for the dogs: Even if we are going just two to three miles close to home, I carry no less than three liters and I do go through most of that. Two, the temperature: The rocks in the southwest tend to reflect the heat, so even when it's a cool seventy-five degrees, it can be much hotter for the dogs, who are closer to the ground. The max temps I will take them out in direct sunlight is seventy-five to eighty degrees. Cloud cover and water play an important factor in this also. Three, the landscape: Elevation change, on- or off-trail, etc.—I have older dogs, so I am thinking of this more and more. I try to take into account the ability of each dog. Four, first aid: I always carry a first-aid kit and a rescue harness as well. I've used it two or three times. Finally, snake training: This is super important for any dog in the southwest. All my dogs have had it. It's been involuntarily tested on the trail and proven worth it.

There are a lot of times when I just feel meh, but then I think, *No, I need to get out for the dogs*. I set out to find places where there are no people and where my dogs can be dogs. In doing so, we've explored Arizona from top to bottom, and I've found some of the most amazing places. I also seek out water for them because it's so warm here. Because of that, I've gotten to know which streams flow at which times and how much rainfall a place gets. My knowledge of the landscape has grown so much through my dogs.

I don't think I ever would have searched to find them without my dogs as motivation. I just love it: They're able to experience life and be dogs and run free. It's worth the extra research and trouble.

—*@goldentrailz*

All five dogs with the Superstition Wilderness in the background, on one of many morning hikes close to home.

OSA, JASPER & KELSEY

An instant bond between dogs leads to a life of adventure.

I had been volunteering at the Oregon Humane Society for about a year, walking dogs. It was a really rewarding experience. I had a dog, Sadie, at home already. She was getting a little older, and her walks were getting shorter, so I had the energy to give to shelter pets. I told myself I wasn't looking for another dog—though, of course, you're always looking, right?

I made good on that for about a year. But then I walked past one kennel and saw these big, mesmerizing glacial-blue eyes and I stopped in my tracks.

All the dogs had little cards next to them with their information, temperament, and history. I saw that Osa was about two years old and that she had lived on the streets for a while. She was picked up at a shelter in California and had been on the list to be euthanized. The Humane Society brought her up to Oregon with a Second Chance program, and she was adopted into another family, but it wasn't a good fit. They had her for about six months or so before they surrendered her.

Osa sat back in the corner of the kennel and seemed very timid, but she had that one slow little tail flick, where you could tell that she was interested in me. I very cautiously approached, unlatched her lock, went in, and

ABOVE: Osa, Jasper, and Kelsey doing what they love the most: getting far away, together, in the Oregon backcountry.

OPPOSITE: Jasper and Osa partake in their favorite pastime: sibling wrestling.

sat down. Within a few seconds, she walked right up to me, circled into my lap, just went full doggy donut, and lay there. That was it for me. I didn't stand a chance.

Osa came home with me, and we just had the best lives together. And then, unfortunately, Sadie passed away from a pretty sudden, aggressive form of cancer.

Sadie was part malamute, which is a beautiful but notoriously challenging breed. I knew that I was familiar with their special requirements, and I felt capable enough to seek out another one that I could care for. I found a breed-specific rescue up in Washington. But

again, I was thinking, *Oh, I've got Osa and we're loving our lives together.*

But I kept an eye on this rescue's site, always refreshing their adoption page. Then one day, a profile for a ten-year-old malamute-husky mix named Jasper popped up. It turned out that he had spent his life tied up in somebody's backyard. Malamutes are a lot of work, and someone took on more than they could handle with him and decided that tying him up was the way they were going to try to fit him into their life. Luckily for all of us, they recognized that that wasn't the right situation and surrendered him.

Out of dozens of applications, I was picked to come meet Jasper. So Osa and I drove one hundred and something miles. She went up there as a solo dog, and I told her if the meeting went well, we'd talk about it.

I opened the car door and it was instant: They were brother and sister. Osa's always been standoffish and submissive, but all of a sudden, it was like she said, "I'm big sister." She jumped all over Jasper—I've never seen her behave like that with any dog before or since.

So she picked him, really. She said, "Load him in the back. He's coming with us." And here we are, many years later.

Osa is funny. She's always had that sort of wise, sage kind of presence, where you feel like she knows more than she'll let on. She's incredibly sensitive and in tune with everybody's energy around her, whereas Jasper

Standing on the edge of it all, deep in the heart of Utah's red rock country.

is our constant jester. He's a total wild-child juggernaut. We always say people need to have soft knees around him because he comes barreling into the room and you have to be ready or he'll lay you down.

I could have never imagined two creatures that come from such different backgrounds and have such different personalities being so in love with each other. It's been really remarkable to witness. It makes me think about, on a grander scale, all of us, and how we can fit together like puzzle pieces that don't make any sense, but we find a way to make it work.

Both dogs, by nature, need quite a bit of exercise, stimulation, and attention. I knew that they were going to need long walks and long runs. But on the seven-hundredth neighborhood walk, when we were trying to get the miles in and take the edge off a little, I just kind of thought, *What if I gave them more?*

After that, we started hiking together. I've always loved the outdoors and have always been a hiker myself, and my partner and I had taken Sadie hiking. But for Osa and Jasper, nature became this space where their challenges in their past lives seemed to melt away. Osa especially lacked a lot of confidence when we first brought her home. She was really anxious in a lot of situations. And in the outdoors, those walls that she had built up because she had had so many people let

I could have never imagined two creatures that come from such different backgrounds and have such different personalities being so in love with each other.

her down before, they just crumbled away. It was almost as though us returning her to a space where she could be free was, for her, the ultimate lesson in trust.

We've found that in those open, wild spaces, they can be who they were always meant to be—who I never would have known they could be had I not asked the question, *What if I could give them more?*

Osa is an expert at sniffing out the shady spots for prime napping when desert camping.

We've only scratched the surface in Montana. I have a fond memory of us outside of the limits of Glacier National Park. I was sitting drinking my morning coffee when I realized a nearby bush was moving. I walked over and realized it was Osa and Jasper. They decided no one had given them a treat in a minute, so like the little team they are, they had snuck away and were picking fresh huckleberries, one by one, as an adventure snack.

We love spaces like these where we all can feel free; it just really feels like a return to all of our primitive selves—a return to nature for them and for ourselves.

These dogs are made for the road. The sound of an engine is like a lullaby. The second they climb in the truck, they're asleep before I leave the driveway. They know we're getting in the car not to drive to the vet or to a daycare where I'm going to leave them; we're going because we're about to go explore together.

Our grandest adventure, where we really kind of fell into this life of doing more than just day hikes or weekend camping trips, was when we drove them to Alaska in our little truck bed camper—it's the smallest one you can get. We crammed all our big bodies in there together and spent days hiding from mosquitoes, all piled on top of

ABOVE: Jasper's eternal expression: "Where to next?"

OPPOSITE: Relaxing on scorched earth outside Fields, Oregon.

Our first adventures started out with a couple of hikes and a couple of peaks, then we just kept building. Last fall, we hiked the tallest peak in New Mexico, and that felt special—it's not a tremendously high peak in the world of mountains, but it sounded really cool! We did the same thing in Utah.

each other. We made it work. Being close to each other and far away from everything else is our happiest place.

The first time I took them camping by myself, I went to a campground that was just under an hour away. I pulled in and realized I had forgotten my tent and the stove. So I turned around, went back home, picked those things up, and went back to the campground. I always look back on that experience as having given myself an opportunity to not do it perfectly. I had the chance to make mistakes and not feel like they were such *big* mistakes that I couldn't continue with what I'd set out to do. You do that trip, that one overnight, and then you feel more prepared and more excited about trying two nights, and it continues to grow.

In January 2022, I drove them to Mexico. They've eaten tacos on the coast of Mexico under a palapa. I never would have imagined myself driving to Mexico—it just seemed far away, and the distance could pose challenges that I might not be ready

for. But the idea of being able to give them these experiences makes me feel strong and makes me feel ready to face whatever challenges come. Watching the dogs splash around on a beach in Mexico with dolphins flipping around in the surf right behind them is something I'll never forget. We're so lucky to live this life of adventure together.

—*@kelseykagan*

We've found that in those open, wild spaces, they can be who they were always meant to be.

BELOW: A windblown Jasper, perched on fallen rocks on the shores of Lake Mead, Nevada.

OPPOSITE: A breathtaking sunset in wildflower season, above the tree line in the Coast Range.

LOKI & SARI

A mischievous dog lives up to his name—and changes his human's life in the process.

I had gotten a new job that I had difficulty adapting to, and I had just moved out on my own into a little studio apartment. I was pretty lonely. I knew nothing about dogs, but I had a feeling that a dog would probably help my life a lot. Call it intuition. I put up an ad online saying I was looking for a puppy, preferably a mixed breed. Someone replied that they just had a litter, so I drove an hour outside Montreal to this little farm and picked out Loki.

The next few weeks were tough, because Loki was a very high-energy, pretty dominant, and super smart little puppy. But then I started researching as much as I could and reading books and articles online. I went to a dog park where, thankfully, I met people who knew dogs, so I would ask questions of as many people as I could, and they would tell me to try this training technique, or to train him a certain way.

The next few months were a huge learning experience for me. I was trying to manage working full-time and having a puppy and everything that goes with that. But I kept researching, trying to understand dog psychology. Lots of trial and error. I ended up learning a lot about dogs in general, and I

ABOVE: Tongue all the way out while hiking one of the seven peaks of Mont-Vallières-de-Saint-Réal in Québec.

OPPOSITE: Another shot from Mont-Vallières-de-Saint-Réal. A hiking break means more Loki photos.

I have this 24/7, always-ready adventure companion.

Loki is extremely smart. When he was a puppy, sometimes he'd steal food because I didn't understand yet which places he could access and which he couldn't. When he was home alone, he'd steal something and go hide it. When I got home, I didn't even know any food was gone. But then three hours later, Loki would look at me, go to his hiding spot, and pull out a piece of bread and start munching on it. He's very resourceful, and he's very mischievous. He lives up to his name, one hundred percent.

Because he's so smart, he needs me to really be on his ass for everything, for lack of a better phrase. I can't let him get away with anything, or else he'll get away with

ABOVE: At the top of Mont Kaaikop, Québec. Loki's a natural when it comes to posing for the camera.

RIGHT: It's mandatory for Loki to swim in every body of water he encounters.

was able to train Loki. Everybody always says he's so social and so well-behaved, and I say, "Well, it took a lot of work."

I got Loki DNA tested. He has several breeds in him: Northern Inuit, Czechoslovakian wolfdog, husky, German shepherd, Australian shepherd, Australian cattle dog, a bit of malamute, and who knows what else. He has a lot of energy, and he needs a lot of mental stimulation too.

everything. He always tries to push his boundaries. It's helped make me a more firm and assertive person.

Loki also loves cuddling—on his terms. At certain times of the day—when he's exhausted, for example—he'll come up beside me and just put his paw on me and say, "Now's your time to pet me." If I stop, he looks at me, then puts his paw on me again and says, "We're not done here yet." He can occasionally be very demanding. I don't mind it.

Every dog owner is going to say their dog isn't like other dogs, but even other dog owners tell me Loki has so much personality. He's quirky.

At first, hiking with Loki was tough because it was all new to me. He's almost seventy pounds, and he likes to pull a lot. When we're going up, it's fun, but on the way down—it's not very fun! But then I started asking other dog owners, "What do you do? What do you use for this? How do you train them to do this?" and it became a community thing, where I was always asking questions and learning more. The more I talked to people, the more I realized how energetic Loki is compared to most dogs, and the more I realized that we could do really big hikes without me having to worry about exhausting him. Because Loki is always ready to go.

When you see him at home, you'd think he has no energy whatsoever. But once we're in the forest, something clicks and he's just going for three, four, five hours nonstop. One summer we did seven peaks in a row, and he was just ready to keep going. He's super alert. He has a high prey drive—God forbid he's not on a leash when he sees a squirrel. He's extremely food driven, too, so sometimes we'll just be hiking and all of a sudden his nose hits the ground, and he'll go off into the forest and come out with a piece of bread or something else edible. (It happens a lot—you'd be surprised.)

I'd always done small hikes here and there, but he gave me a reason to look for bigger hikes—and then I realized how much I liked them. City life can get a bit draining, but when Loki and I go out in nature for a weekend, I come back and feel reenergized. Loki allowed me to discover a side of myself that I kind of knew was always there but not

Sunsets are a thing of beauty on the Gaspésie coastline in Québec.

BELOW: The stick collector. Loki loves pulling out logs from lakes and chewing on them.

RIGHT: Loki looks at the path ahead on the Swaggin trail, which overlooks a river by the same name.

to what extent; he's helped me learn to what degree I really enjoy hiking and camping.

I have this 24/7, always-ready adventure companion. Being with him allowed me to find more comfort in my own solitude and doing things that I want to do, as opposed to trying to fit in and do what other people want to do.

Loki just changed my life for the better.

I also find it's easier to go hiking, in the sense that people are much friendlier when you have a dog—for the most part—as opposed to when you're hiking by yourself and people look at you like, *Wow, that's kind of weird.* Especially where I live in Quebec, when you go outside Montreal, I find as an immigrant that it's not always very immigrant-friendly, to put it lightly. Sometimes, even though I'll say, "Hi, how are you?" people can be very cold, but once they see the dog, it breaks the ice.

Loki has allowed me to want to go hiking in places where maybe I wouldn't have gone before. I feel motivated to go to places farther away too. We've been to Gaspésie three years in a row now, every summer, which is about seven hours away from Montreal. It's very touristy, but it's also by the Atlantic Ocean, so you can go up mountains and see breathtaking views of the ocean. Honestly, I know if I didn't have Loki, I probably wouldn't go.

It gives me a sort of excitement and thrill, just the sense of fulfillment of seeing him enjoying himself and sharing these moments with me. There are so many places I want to take him. Most importantly, I hope to take him on a European hiking trip to Switzerland and Germany in a few years' time.

Loki has even gotten me out hiking in the winter, which is something I would have never done in my life—you couldn't have convinced me. I hated winter. Before, I would have stayed cooped up all day. But now I'm a winter person. I go to the dog park when it's cold outside. I've learned to dress appropriately and get the right layers. And Loki and I go hiking, which makes winters more fun.

When we're not adventuring, we have a little routine. I have two shifts—one in the morning and one in the evening. In the morning, sometimes Loki comes with me, but sometimes he wants to sleep in. He always comes with me at night. We take walks, and every single day from 1:30 to 2:30 p.m. we go to the dog park so Loki can have his social time with his clique of five or six dogs who have known him since he was a puppy. Then, on weekends, we schedule hikes.

When I first got Loki I wasn't doing great from a mental health point of view. It'd been

a year with ups and downs—but a lot more downs than ups. Loki forced me to take him out for an hour every day to the dog park, he made me stick to a routine, and we had to socialize. He definitely helped me to get out of bed and get outside on days when I did not want to. The routine has benefitted us both.

Loki just changed my life for the better. He allowed me to be more myself and be more comfortable being on my own. I've done things and been to places I probably never would have gone if not for him. It's really ignited my love for the outdoors to the point where I'll even base my next six months on where I want to go—like I want to go to Europe to go hiking, which I would have never even thought of before. It gives me something to look forward to.

—*@sarisubzero*

Always wearing a smile, no matter the elevation.

OLLIE & ALY

Nineteen states down, a lifetime of adventures to go.

My dream dog was always a Red Tri-Australian shepherd, but I felt like there were too many dogs in the world that needed a good home and couldn't justify the expense. I was on a mission to find a rescue or one from a farm. I knew I'd find my pup; it was just a matter of time.

Everyone in my life had their radars on to help me find the perfect pup. One day, my mom sent me a Facebook post from her friend's aunt in Missouri saying she had a litter of Australian shepherd puppies that she was practically giving away. They had three left, and one was Ollie. When I saw his photo, I immediately knew he was mine. I was living in New York City at the time, so I rented a car, grabbed my good friend William, and drove sixteen hours to Missouri to pick up my new best friend.

I was worried whether Ollie was going to like me or not, since we didn't get to meet in person before I picked him up. We FaceTimed ahead of time, though, and he licked the screen, so clearly that meant he wanted to be my best friend for life. When we finally met in person, it was instant love. He cuddled right up and melted into my arms. He had the cutest little silly personality. We've been inseparable ever since.

ABOVE: Resting after a seven-mile hike on the Cadillac South Ridge Trail in Acadia National Park, Maine.

OPPOSITE: Exploring the Samuel H. Boardman State Scenic Corridor, Oregon.

If we're together, he's having a blast.

People were surprised that I got a dog while living in a New York apartment. The hardest thing was walking up and down five flights of stairs for potty training, but other than that, it was not bad!

Ollie is a city pup in the sense that he will take a poo on the sidewalk no problem, but he gets most excited when I ask him if he wants to go on an adventure. I put his bandana on and he takes off to the car, ready to go explore. Whether it's a camping trip, walking around a new city, or climbing in a boulder field, he is happy and always down! If we're together, he's having a blast. A true adventure pup!

ABOVE: First time getting to run around off-leash through a field in Chatham, New York. One happy doggo.

OPPOSITE: Exploring Otter Cliffs, Thunder Hole, Sand Beach, and Gorham Mountain in Acadia National Park.

trips was our three-week road trip from LA to Seattle, hiking the coast. I'm a photographer, so I was taking photos along the way, but when we stopped in Brookings, Oregon, I was really excited to capture this perfect shot at Samuel H. Boardman State Scenic Corridor that we would have to hike down to (though I wasn't exactly sure where it was). We were hiking alone on a rainy, misty morning on questionable terrain that was extremely muddy and difficult to navigate. All of a sudden, Ollie saw a squirrel, got excited, and took off running, causing us both to slip since he was on leash. We started sliding down a cliff that dropped off into the Pacific Ocean. Luckily, I was able to grab some roots and pull us back up, but I really thought that might be the end for a second there.

He keeps me present and reminds me to appreciate the little moments in life.

ABOVE: Hanging out in Central Park. Just a typical day in NYC.

OPPOSITE: Ollie's first time camping in Boulder, Colorado.

Ollie hikes all terrains. He can hike across big boulders and jump as far or as high as he needs to make it across. When there's water, you can bet he is going to jump in and swim. He is a little athlete! He really appreciates being outside in nature with his people.

Our bucket list is to visit all fifty states in his lifetime. So far, we are at nineteen.

Ollie and I have been on many trips together, but one of our most memorable

I work from home, so Ollie and I are never really apart for long, and on the weekends we spend most of our time exploring together. Some of my happiest moments in life are ones spent with Ollie. Our morning walks, our adventures, afternoon cuddles—as long as we're together, we're happy. He keeps me present and reminds me to appreciate the little moments in life. Ollie is my best friend. I thank God every day for bringing us together. I love my little Wiggle Butt.

—@aly_pentangelo

FALL

HOW PERFECT is a crisp hike among fall foliage? The orange, red, and gold hues make for a spectacular backdrop for adventure (and photos!). Heading to a peak can offer breathtaking bird's-eye views of the trees as they turn. And as the leaves change, so do the trails. Fewer people are out, which means more nature for you and your dog. Pack a dog sweater or two, camp out, and get cozy as the calendar year falls away.

BELOW: Riley is the best companion for outdoor adventures. She's always eager to hit the trails, especially in the cooler autumn months when she can dive into the leaves for fun!

OPPOSITE: Skipper at his local park during the fall.

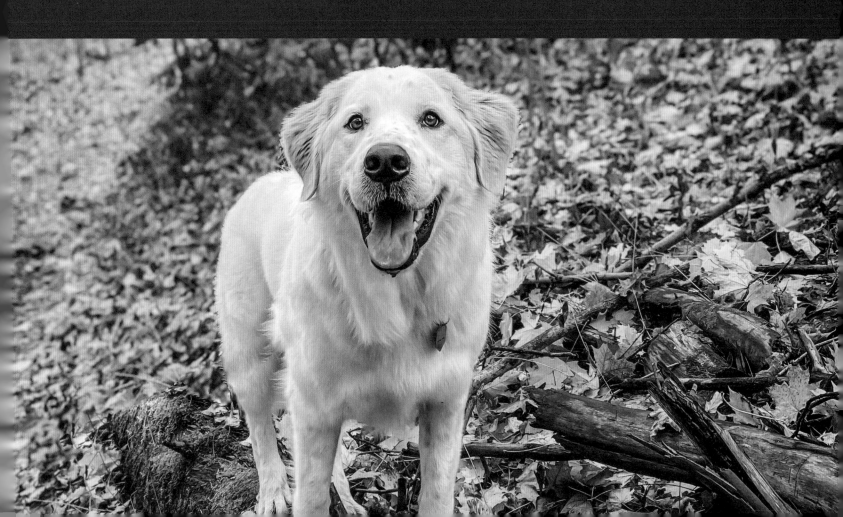

OLLIE & SARAH

Whether they're paddleboarding or getting a PhD, this puppy is always by her human's side.

I was living in Vancouver for grad school, getting my PhD in geology. At that point, I'd been there for four or five years without a dog, and I was starting to get to the point where I just needed a dog. I realized I couldn't just pet the department dogs anymore; I needed my own dog to love me and go on adventures with me. I was thinking about

leaving the city because it wasn't as dog-friendly as people had said it was, and I ended up getting a job back in my home province of Alberta. As soon as I got my job acceptance letter, I said, "I am going to get a dog." That was the first item on my need-to-buy list. It wasn't furniture for my apartment. It was: I need to get a dog.

I looked at rescuing a dog, but I was moving into a condo, and a lot of rescues had rules requiring fenced-in backyards. So

I decided to go the route of a breeder. I wanted an Aussie, and I found a breeder in my hometown of Edmonton. The first thing I did when I decided to move back was to get a deposit for a future puppy.

I had my deposit on another puppy, a boy that I was going to name Ollie. My mom even made me a little dog dish at pottery class that said "Ollie" on it. But two days before I was supposed to pick him up, the

ABOVE: Ice walking at Maligne Canyon in Jasper, Alberta, Canada, to view the frozen waterfalls and karsted limestone features. Ollie found a log jam and was trying to rescue this frozen stick.

OPPOSITE: Paddleboarding on Rundle Forebay in Canmore, Alberta. On hot days she likes to swim alongside the board to cool off!

shy and reserved. But the next day, it was like she said, "Okay, this is my new home. Good luck, everybody!"

We used to call her Tooth Tornado because she would bite at everything. She was chompy, but most puppies are, and she eventually grew out of that. I think it was because she started going to daycare and another dog bit her and then she realized, "Whoa, that hurts. Maybe I shouldn't do that." Ever since that point, she's never bitten me again. But that puppy stage was really scary; she was like a little land shark.

I don't want to give her a bad rap! She's nice now. She is a very empathetic, sweet little girl. She just loves being around people and dogs. She's very outgoing and very loving. No more biting.

ABOVE: Hiking the Big Beehive in Lake Louise, Alberta. This is one of Ollie's favorite hikes because there is an opportunity for snack breaks at the Lake Agnes Tea House on the way to the top.

RIGHT: Summit naps on Sulphur Skyline trail in Jasper, Alberta. Ollie needed to recharge and save some energy for zooming around in the small stream at the trailhead.

breeder called to tell me he wouldn't make a good apartment dog. She said she had a new litter and that there was a really sweet little girl who would be a good fit for me.

I thought, *Well, I guess a girl can be Ollie too:* Olivia, nicknamed Ollie. So I decided she would be Ollie 2.0—but she ended up being Ollie #1 in my heart.

Ollie was a tiny little terror. I was so afraid of her the first four months I owned her. The second they put her in my arms, I thought, *Oh my God, this is a sweet little bundle of joy,* and when I got her home, she was super

Ollie did her first hike at six months old. I took her to Ink Pots and Johnston Canyon in Banff. She cried the whole way up and the whole way down. I carried her part of the way because I realized it might have been a bit too ambitious. I thought, *Well, we can only go up from here.*

After that, we started going out on smaller hikes, especially near where my parents live, in Kelowna, British Columbia, since there are a lot of little trails around there. Then Ollie realized that there was a whole new range of scents for her to smell, and she didn't have to walk on pavement and there were no distractions.

Solo trips—just the two of us—are my favorite ones to do with her.

Now, if you say, "We're going hiking," she gets really excited and runs to the door, waiting for her harness to be put on. She knows, and she loves going out.

Last summer, we went camping in Jasper together. It was the first time Ollie decided that she was going to be okay on the

Sulphur Skyline trail in Jasper, Alberta. This is one of Ollie and Sarah's favorite dog-friendly trails in Jasper National Park. The summit offers incredible panoramic views of the Canadian Rockies and is a preferred napping spot for Ollie!

paddleboard. She sat right at the front and had her little feet dangling in the water. Everyone who passed us asked, "How did you train her to do that?" And I just said, "I don't know. She's never done this before!"

I paddled us over to a secluded beach. We had lunch there, and she splashed in the water and played with her sticks. Then we paddled back to the car and went to our favorite dog-friendly brewery and had a beer. That night, we hung out by the campfire together.

Everywhere I can take her, I try to.

Solo trips—just the two of us—are my favorite ones to do with her. I find it's when we have the best bonding opportunities. You don't have to focus on having conversations with other people. You just get to hang out with your dog and see how much they enjoy what they're doing.

Nature is Ollie's happy place. When we go on walks around the neighborhood, she's happy to roll around in the grass. But as soon as she sees we're on a hiking trail, for the first kilometer, she just has the zoomies. She's beyond happy. Nature is where she goes to have fun, and it's where she knows that we're going to spend the whole day together. I'm not going to be distracted by my work or anything else. Ollie knows that day is all about her.

Ollie was my motivation to finish grad school. I was getting to the point where I wondered if it was worth it; I couldn't see where my future was going. But once I got Ollie, I could see how much of my happiness came from her. I felt motivated to finish grad school and stop paying tuition so I could buy Ollie a house with a backyard someday.

She would come to the geology lab and look at rocks with me. Sometimes she was allowed to come out for fieldwork with me too. So I put her little backpack on her and I let her carry a sample or two. The first conference she went to with me was when she was ten weeks old. My presentation was over two days, and some people at the lab told me she could stay in their offices if she needed a break from the table. News of her spread like wildfire. People were asking, "Have you been to the puppy table yet?" If someone came by and she wasn't there, they'd say to me, "Oh, I thought there was supposed to be a puppy here." My presentation won that year, and all my coworkers tease me that it was because of Ollie.

When I graduated, I asked my supervisor if Ollie could get an honorary degree because I wouldn't have finished without her. He said no! But my whole PhD thesis is dedicated to her, and the last paragraph of the acknowledgments is for her.

Ollie wasn't allowed to come to the actual graduation ceremony, but my advisor let her stay in his office until it was over. She came out for cake, pizza, and pictures.

She even had a little grad cap. I have photos of her wearing it next to me when I had my PhD regalia on.

Everywhere I can take her, I try to. I'm one of those people.

The way I think about it, I would hate for her to think that her life just has to be waiting for me at the house and never anything more than a quick walk around the block. That makes me sad because she deserves to have a really good life too. So she gets to come with me whenever she can.

—*@ollie.wagon*

BELOW: Hiking to Raven's End at Yamnuska in Kananaskis Country, Alberta.

OPPOSITE LEFT: Goofing around while kayaking on Pyramid Lake in Jasper, Alberta. Ollie sometimes likes to assist with paddling when she thinks she and her human aren't going fast enough or in the correct direction.

OPPOSITE RIGHT: Ollie wearing her grad cap at convocation.

RILEY & LEANNA

A walk around the neighborhood leads to a life of outdoor adventure when a woman meets her perfect dog.

met Riley in December 2019, just before the world started to get a little bit crazy. I wasn't planning on getting a dog, but I had seen photos of these puppies online, and she stole my heart. The rest of her littermates were all golden, and she was the only puppy that was white with golden ears. I decided to go meet the puppies—I did not tell my partner,

Adam, that I brought a deposit with me—and we instantly fell in love with Riley.

Riley's kind of like a human. She's very, very cuddly. She loves human affection. She likes to be around humans more than dogs; we're like her pack. She's so sweet. We've worked very hard with her training, so she listens very well. I sound like I have the perfect dog—but she *is* really good!

She's my little shadow, my best friend. She goes everywhere with me. I think incorporating her into everyday activities has made her a very calm and socialized dog. She's not very reactive toward other dogs, and she's really good with people. I also speak to her in full sentences. I know some people just tell their dogs "no" or give just one word here or there, but I feel like speaking to her in

ABOVE: Riley's favorite season? Winter! She was definitely made for Canadian winters and it's impossible to keep her inside.

OPPOSITE: After a swim in the lake, Riley's humans brought her over to the canoes and kayaks so she could get familiar with them. They were eager to bring her out on the water, but it was important to get her used to them while on land first!

"If I walk out onto this log, they won't know I'm actually going to jump in the lake for a swim."
—Riley, definitely

sentences has made her very intelligent. She understands a lot of what we say.

Prior to Riley, I was not a very active person or someone who went camping. My work got shut down for almost a year, due to the pandemic. A lot of our hiking began because we were bored during the day. We did 5k walks every morning and night, and then I got sick of walking on the pavement and decided to go and explore somewhere new every day. I would drive to our local conservation areas and explore our provincial parks.

Riley loved it. There was lots of wildlife for her to observe and new smells for mental stimulation. She loves to try to chase bunnies and squirrels at any given opportunity.

She's my little shadow, my best friend.

Her natural instincts definitely come out when we're hiking and camping. She's a Great Pyrenees and a golden retriever mix. She is always on alert. When we camp, she has a fifty-foot line that we put her on and we just let her do her thing. She likes to dive into the brush and pop back out, watch the squirrels and the birds, and lay by the fire at night!

If you tell Riley we're going camping in the trailer, she goes crazy. She's so excited. (Right now, she's looking at me like, "Oh, you said trailer?!")

I pack more for Riley than I do for myself and Adam. She has her own sleeping bag. The dining table in the trailer folds down into a bed, so that becomes Riley's bed and she sleeps there. We have her basket full of her toys so she can go and grab whatever she wants to play with. It's a small trailer, so we're not in there most of the time—it's mostly for sleeping or if it's raining. It's the perfect travel trailer for our adventures.

We want to travel all over with her—that's why we ended up getting the trailer, to go

TOP: Riley's first time in a canoe and first time at Bon Echo Provincial Park in Ontario, Canada.

RIGHT: Riley and Leanna love to hike during snowstorms. Here, they climbed to the top of the mountain at Mono Cliff's Provincial Park in Ontario.

When we're not camping, we have a set routine. Riley wakes me up every morning by 8 a.m. If I'm not awake, she's standing over me, breathing on me. Every day, we do our morning and evening 5k walks. When we're hanging out at home, Riley likes to bark at the mailman—he is her archnemesis. She sits and stares out the window, waiting for him to come so she can bark at him. She also spends her time playing with our senior Shih Tzu, Dottie. They're really cute together, they love to play and they give each other kisses before bed.

Adventuring with your dog is so fulfilling. There's enrichment for your dog *and* yourself, just being outside and breathing in the fresh air

ABOVE: There's nothing better than exploring and making memories at national and provincial parks.

RIGHT: Beach day! Riley loves to cool off and play in the water.

traveling with Riley instead of leaving her home. We're excited to bring her to the east coast of Canada, like New Brunswick, Nova Scotia, and Prince Edward Island. That's where my family is from, and I know she would enjoy it. Next year, we're hoping to do the west coast. Hopefully, the year after that, we can go to some of the national parks in the States.

Riley has walked on the ocean floor! She's pictured here at Hopewell Rocks Provincial Park in New Brunswick, Canada.

Go outside and explore with your dogs.

and exploring new places. It's definitely given me a new appreciation for the outdoors, and it's motivated me to want to go explore new places.

Prior to having Riley and going on our adventures, I was pretty high maintenance. I was always done up. Now, I'm a totally different person. I give a lot of credit to Riley because,

honestly, instead of going out, I'd rather be at home hanging out with her or going for a hike. That's what I truly find enjoyable.

Go outside and explore with your dogs. Don't keep them cooped up all day. Getting out makes their life better, it makes *your* life better. I may have other dogs in this lifetime, but we are the only family Riley will ever know. I feel like I need to give her my one hundred and ten percent and the best life possible.

—*@riley.goldenpyr*

BEAR & AMBREEN

A shocking discovery inspires one small-dog owner to give her pup the biggest life possible.

In January 2020, I adopted Bear from a nearby shelter that's extremely popular because they tend to get smaller dogs. I'm a small-dog person—they just have so much personality—and I have a rule that I will only get a dog I can carry in case of emergency.

A lot of the dogs you see at shelters are frantic or heartbreakingly eager, or they're older and give you a look that says, *Keep walking.* Bear, though, was perched on his little cot and barked at me just once—it was so sassy. He was advertised as being three years old and some sort of a Shih Tzu mix. I immediately thought, *This is the one.*

After I got him, these strange health problems started happening. He lost a tooth. He was trembling a lot. His eyes were really cloudy. We went to the vet because I didn't think any of it was normal. I was so alarmed—he was only three years old, and losing a tooth out of nowhere is startling. I thought it could be something congenital.

After several hundreds of dollars and many tests, the vet said, "There's good news and there's bad news." The bad news was that Bear was actually ten. The good news was that all these health problems were very normal for a senior dog. He has so much

ABOVE: Bear watches Ambreen prepare his breakfast. He won't eat plain kibble unless and until she adds freshly cooked meat to it.

OPPOSITE: Bear hates the rain and puts up a good fight against wearing his raincoat, but he never wins.

Nobody is guaranteed tomorrow, especially not dogs.

energy—you'd never think he was ten years old. But everything started falling into place after that.

At first, it was really shocking. But then I just became so sad. I knew I wouldn't have adopted him had I known he was ten. It's a terrible reality, but getting an older dog is financially and emotionally scary. There are many unpredictable financial responsibilities that come with that time of their lives. I was also afraid of getting emotionally attached and not knowing how much longer he had to live.

I went through all of this processing and finally I realized this: My thoughts are selfish. Nobody is guaranteed tomorrow, especially not dogs. Bear fits into my life so well and exactly the way that he is. I would just have to start making some adjustments.

Bear is a firecracker. This is his house; I just live in it. He guards the entire neighborhood. You can't be in your garden if Bear's around. My neighbors call him the sheriff.

He is so particular about things. He does not like to be handled. If I touch him too much, he will get up and move and sit just out of my reach. Now that I'm teleworking full time, he rarely has days when he's alone

and I truly believe that there are times when he's thinking, *Please, just send me back to the shelter. This is too much people time for me.* I'm always saying, "Love me, love me! Be with me!" I laugh at how needy I've become for his affection because he rejects me so shamelessly.

His personality is absolutely that of a very entitled elderly man who has done his duty for this country and is not going to take any more nonsense from anybody else. Bear barks at me when he wants food. He never licks me out of affection, nor does he whine for attention. He barks at me when he wants to play with his toy or to go out, and he wants to be outside all the time. I only see him when I force him to come inside.

But he's a fantastic creature. There's absolutely no way, as a single person, I could have made it through the pandemic without him.

Unfortunately, he has a whole life story behind him that I know nothing about. Whatever he's been through has shaped his fear of certain places and things. I don't think he was

ABOVE: Bear cooling off at a dog beach at Quiet Waters in Annapolis, Maryland.

OPPOSITE TOP: Bear on his first boat ride. He was not a fan and will not do it again.

OPPOSITE BOTTOM: Bear at the start of a city park hiking trail. He loves hiking.

ever exposed to public places like stores and shopping areas. He also hates car rides.

He's extremely scared of large dogs, but his fear comes out in aggression. He barks and lunges when a big dog walks by, and every once in a while, whatever smack he's talking sets off one of those dogs and they come at us. In general, I'll pick him up when I see a large dog coming our way, but every once in a while, we turn a corner and I can't act fast enough. Unfortunately, I have had to pry him out of the mouths of bigger dogs more than a few times.

A few months ago, we ended up in the ER because a dog pulled out of her owner's hands and charged us. Before I could pick up Bear, she grabbed him by the neck and shook. I was terrified. It was a very long night in the ER.

When we finally left, with antibiotics for his wounds, as we were walking, Bear started barking at a husky. I swear: It will never stop. It's who he is.

Bear is an extreme guard dog, which I found out when I took him camping *once*. We did not sleep that night. Anytime he heard a sound, he was barking—barking at the birds, barking at a twig snapping. He couldn't relax. But Bear is fantastic with hiking.

I have always been a city girl. In fact, I've only lived in apartments my whole life. Now that my job is fully telework, I've gotten so much of my life back and a lot of things fell into place, so I bought a property in the suburbs of DC. My townhouse is lakefront, and there's a beautiful trail around the lake. Bear just came alive when we moved here. Every day, weather permitting, we walk around the lake, and it's so lovely. There's also a lot of wildlife here. Bear has gained so much confidence that when he sees a deer, he'll try to hunt it down. He even took off after a vulture, leaping as if he could reach it in the air. If the geese come too close, he will give them the business too. He's in his element here.

ABOVE: Bear waiting to be let out to the backyard, where he'll assume his post as watchman of the neighborhood.

OPPOSITE: A hot Bear in the summer.

When we're not walking around our lake, we usually hike the trails at Rock Creek Park, which cuts right across DC and goes into Maryland and Virginia. But I'm always thinking about where we can go explore that will be good for Bear.

I've always had small dogs, so I know you need to be able to tell a dog's signs of exhaustion and make decisions based on those—versus looking to the dog to tell you that they need a break, because they're not always going to do so. Bear will go until he's at that point of exhaustion and that's not good for a senior dog with joint problems. So I know I need to watch him and decide when to pick him up and put him in a backpack or when we need to take a break. I'm also very mindful that Bear is exercising more than usual on our hiking days, so I give him extra protein and keep him hydrated in different ways, like adding broth to his food. And because of his age, I am far more involved in planning everything ahead of time.

Obviously, since Bear's getting older, he's slowed down a lot. But I would not want to stop living life and stay indoors no matter what age I was, and I want to make sure he

has the best lifestyle I can provide where he keeps exploring. So don't stop adventuring just because you have an older dog. Find ways to still get out there. There are so many tools and gadgets out there to help solve a lot of these problems. Cooling vests were a game-changer for us with the heat, for example. Learning to connect with other dog owners and ask questions has been really helpful, and empowering as well.

Learning of Bear's true body age changed the way I treated him. I often think about the reality that I have fallen so deeply in love with my dog at a point where he has likely lived most of his life already. While that makes me sad, it's also made me extremely intentional with the time that we spend together. I want him to experience everything in life.

I've been blessed with this surprise, and Bear has taught me a lot. He is who he is. It's his life to live; he shares it with me. It would be selfish of me to try to make him something he's not. It would be selfish of me to say, "Well, he's lived this much of his life this way, but I want a dog who's going to give me more."

As we both learn about each other, what's been fantastic for us is for me to accept him for who he is and work with or around that personality. There are behavioral things Bear and I can work on, certainly. But at some point, I have to respect his autonomy.

Before Bear, I'd always had younger dogs, and that relationship is so training-focused that I feel we forget these creatures actually come with their own personalities. A dog truly flourishes when you find that perfect balance between nurturing, discipline, and accepting them for who they are.

—@brownpeoplecamping

Bear enjoying a lazy afternoon in his and Ambreen's new home, wondering why she keeps taking things out of boxes rather than taking him on a walk.

Don't stop adventuring just because you have an older dog. Find ways to still get out there.

SKIPPER & CHRISTY

A grieving pair find solace in the healing power of nature.

Skipper was one year old when I met him. He was living with my ex and his extended family, and their three male indoor cats. Skipper was the only dog, and he didn't know anything but what the cats did. He actually learned to wash his paws just like the cats after each meal and outside break. The cats also showed him how to climb up on things, like the couch.

They would straddle the back of the couch with their back legs, stretch their front legs ahead of them, and sleep that way. So Skipper did the same thing: He slept right up there, straddled on the back of the couch between the cats.

When Skipper was two, I moved in and became part of the family. He gravitated toward me. I think he could sense that I was a dog-friendly human,

and soon I was taking him on all of his walks and taking care of him.

When my ex and I decided to move to our own place, I could tell Skipper was a little bit lonely for someone that looked like him, like he was missing his own kind—the cats weren't enough. One day, when I was running errands and saw my local pet store hosting an adoption event with a rescue organization. They had a chihuahua-Yorkie mix puppy that

ABOVE: Skipper and Christy in the Eastern Sierras during fall at Convict Lake in Mammoth Lakes, California.

OPPOSITE: Skipper in Knights Ferry, California, looking cute on one of his hikes.

Skipper in Big Sur, California, enjoying the sun by the ocean.

was vocal, and Skipper was laid-back and communicated by movement more than sound. They were inseparable. They did everything together—sleeping, eating, going on walks, and just getting into trouble together. And we traveled together too.

On one RV camping trip through Washington, what I call "the dog tax" was born: Whenever we stopped for fast food, we had to get something for the dogs. Skipper loved french fries the most.

Unfortunately, my ex and I eventually decided to end things. When we split, Gilligan was my dog but Skipper technically belonged to my ex and his other family members. Skipper and Gilligan were attached at the hip at that point, and I couldn't leave Skipper behind. So there was a financial transaction and Skipper officially became my dog. Gilligan, Skipper, and I left and found our own place in the Central Valley of California.

looked kind of like Skipper when he was a puppy—brown and black with a little bit of white. I decided I wanted to adopt this dog, but I knew Skipper had to make the final decision. My ex brought Skipper down, and he and the puppy hit it off. So I adopted him and named him Gilligan.

Gilligan and Skipper balanced each other out. Gilligan was high-strung, and Skipper was the calming dog. Gilligan

It was hard for all of us. But then we got bad news on top of it all. Our new vet in California told us that Gilligan had an enlarged heart on the left-hand side, and that he only had six months to one year to live.

He said keeping Gilligan calm and doing calm activities might help prolong his life. We could only take short walks to local parks in town or quick rides in the car to their favorite store; anything else could be too stressful.

Gilligan's health really started to decline in 2014, and at the beginning of 2015, it came to a head when he coughed up blood. I had to leave Skipper at home and take Gilligan to the emergency vet. There was nothing they could do. I had to put him to sleep and send him to doggy heaven.

When I came home, Skipper was like, "Where's Gilligan?" He looked for him everywhere—he'd go to the front door, then to the garage door, searching. Then Skipper started to become vocal, barking at me, getting mad at me, like he was yelling, "Where *is* he?!" He was really hurting.

I knew we both needed some kind of therapy, but I didn't want to do traditional therapy. I knew our walks calmed Skipper, so in the middle of the night, I googled "nature therapy" and, bingo, I read that when you get away from urban life and get into nature, it's so healing, it's calming, and it really helps your mental well-being as well as your physical well-being.

I wasn't sure if Skipper would be into hiking. So I started looking in the foothills area to try something small. I found Knights Ferry. It's by a river and has an 1800s-era, old wooden bridge that goes all the way across it, as well as small trails. I thought, *Okay, let's try this*.

I let Skipper ride up front next to me on the way there and smell out the window to track where we were going. When we arrived, I put his harness on and we started up an access trail with an incline. Skipper started pulling ahead of me, and then he started trying to run. I said, "Wait, we're walking—we're hiking!" But he was so excited, he just wanted to run. He pulled me up the hill all the way, and of course he was sniffing everything and peeing on everything as we went. I said,

Skipper and Christy on a morning hike by the Stanislaus River in Knights Ferry.

Gilligan and Skipper balanced each other out.

"Okay, you're into hiking. I can see that." We started going there every week.

Since then, we've been everywhere. We've chased nature's scenery from sunrise to sunset during spring, summer, fall, and winter. We've been to Knights Ferry and other lakes and trails in the area. We've been to Yosemite, Death Valley, Point Reyes, and Crater Lake. We did a thirty-hour road trip to Crater Lake with a stop at McCloud Falls in Mount Shasta before heading home. We've been up and down the California coast from McWay Falls to Fort Bragg. We've been to Lost Sierra, all throughout the Lake Tahoe area, Ebbetts Pass, Carson Pass, and Sonora Pass. We've traveled through the Eastern Sierras from Bridgeport to Lone Pine.

Our adventures came out of loss and tragedy, and it was healing.

We've chased nature's scenery from sunrise to sunset during spring, summer, fall, and winter.

Skipper's health started to decline in late 2021. Our last trip to Yosemite was in November that year. He used to drag me behind him when we hiked, but now he was walking behind me and barely had enough strength to keep up, and he was losing his eyesight. At the beginning of 2022, he started really losing weight, and losing his balance and more of his eyesight. By early March, I determined that I needed to do a goodbye adventure because the end was that close.

I took him to Knights Ferry so he could smell the wildflowers. I had to carry him to the trail and then put him down so he could sniff. The next day we went to Yosemite. I'd gotten a dog stroller so I could push him around there. When we got to a sunny area, I took him out so he could walk. But he was losing balance even on flat land, so I had to put him back in.

I always put sunglasses on him when it was sunny, so Skipper was in his stroller with his

Skipper on the beach in South Lake Tahoe, California.

shades on, resting his head on the side of it. A group of schoolchildren was there for a trip, and they thought he was the cutest thing.

We were on the walkway in Cook's Meadow, where you can view Yosemite Falls. Even though Skipper couldn't see anything, he looked like he was staring up at the falls. I could tell he was taking in the breeze and the smells.

Skipper was born on April 1, 2003. My ex and I had stayed in touch, and on the morning of April 1, 2022, he came to celebrate Skipper's birthday with us. That same afternoon, we went together to send Skipper to doggy heaven.

Since Skipper's passing, I've only been to a few places: I went back to Yosemite, Little Lakes Valley, and Mammoth Lakes in the Eastern Sierras. In Yosemite, I didn't

allow myself to think or feel. But in Little Lakes Valley, where I'd been with Skipper about three years before, I took some time to process. It was bittersweet to be on that trail—kind of a goodbye in spirit.

Skipper was my best friend. We chased scenery from sunrise to sunset together. Being out in nature really healed us and really brought us together. He was my protector. My best friend. My adventure buddy. My guy who was there for me unconditionally, always. I miss and love him.

—*@beautymajic*

ABOVE: Skipper wearing his shades in the Tahoe National Forest, California.

LEFT: Skipper by a lake in the Sierra Nevada foothills in California.

KAIA & NICOL

Little legs won't stop this corgi from going on big adventures.

Our family pet of seventeen years had passed away, and without a dog in the house it was a little lonely. After a few months, my brother started looking for a dog. Everyone knows about corgis from their internet fame, and my brother was obsessed with their butts.

He did a lot of research and found a corgi breeder. My brother asked me if I wanted to go in half with him on a puppy, and I agreed. We drove up to the breeder to meet Kaia and fell in love with her right away.

My brother ended up moving away to Montreal for work and school. By that point, Kaia had already bonded to me, and I'm a teacher, so I had the time off work to train her. So I paid him out for her. Since then, she and I have just been everywhere together.

Kaia is just this spunky girl. She's dog reactive, so people will say she's sassy. But she's just very independent. If she were a human, she'd be very introverted but very adventurous. She's a bit too brave sometimes—like when she sees a large rock, she'll think she can climb it, but then she won't quite make it and she'll be Mufasa-ing, scrambling to hold on.

ABOVE: After moving to the relatively flat Midwestern state of Missouri, USA, Kaia was absolutely stoked to find rocks to climb up and catch a view of beautiful fall foliage.

OPPOSITE: Kaia smiles proudly at the top of her and Nicol's first challenging hike, Carthew Alderson, traversing 20 kilometers up and down 700 meters of elevation. They had lots of fun exploring different landscapes in such a short period of time, and it was doubly worth it for the tacos after!

Kaia is very food motivated. I think she and I are very alike in that food is everything to us! When we're not on an adventure, she wakes me up at six every morning to get fed, then basically begs for food the rest of the day!

We do a lot of trick training and agility. She loves learning—she's definitely a working dog and likes doing things all the time. Seriously: She barely rests. I remember googling "Is it okay that my dog only sleeps twelve hours?" She's always up. Even if she closes her eyes, if we move a muscle, she's right up with us.

We did neighborhood walks with Kaia as a puppy. Eventually, when she was about five or six months old, she started stopping on our walks. She'd just sploot in the middle of the sidewalk. At first, it was really cute, but then she wouldn't move, or she'd start pulling to go back home.

I asked all these corgi people if they knew what was up with that. A trainer friend told me that it might be because Kaia was bored. So we went to this local hill that's like a mini hike, and she had so much fun—there was more to sniff around! We started going there often, and then we just slowly kept building up the distance and elevation. We conditioned our adventuring with that.

Her first hike was a little earlier than people should probably hike with a puppy.

No autumnal road trip is complete without photos of giant maple leaves.

But on the flip side of all that adventurousness and independence, she's the sweetest little thing too. At night she climbs into my bed and snuggles in between my arms. She's really clingy—she'll get right in there. She's also got major FOMO; she thinks all other dogs need to like her. When we're out with friends, we call her the Fun Police: If their dogs are playing, she'll start barking at them and trying to get in between them. Then if they chase her, it's like the time of her life.

She was about eight or nine months, and there was some decent elevation gain. But she loved it: She rolled in horse poo, ran into a lake—it was amazing. We carried her out, but she loved hiking from the get-go.

From the beginning she was really great with road trips too. Cars are easy for her. She likes looking out the windows—just loves taking in the view. And she can always tell where we are. She can sense when I'm turning

I just want to travel the world with her.

toward home, and she knows it's time to do something if we hit a gravel road.

We recently started flying with her too. Her first flight was a little rocky—she wouldn't stay still and she tried to scratch her way out of her crate. But she's been on eight flights now—we've been to Montreal, up to Yukon, down to California, Missouri,

Canadian autumn is very short-lived, but for a two-week period, the larch trees start glowing a beautiful yellow/ orange. Hike Aretheusa Cirque to find the most beautiful trees!

ABOVE: Believe it or not, Kaia and Nicol happened upon this snowy scene on a warm October afternoon.

OPPOSITE: Originally, Kaia and Nicol had planned just a road trip to Colorado, but they noticed that Utah wasn't that far away. So Kaia got to see the incredible red rock formations, arches, and desert in Moab.

and Colorado—and she's so much better. She just sleeps the whole way. She's really gotten comfortable with her carrier, so much so that even if it's lying around, she'll just jump into it. I think she knows when it's out that an adventure is going to happen.

I really want to go to Italy with her and hike the mountains there. I think anywhere in Europe would be really cool to bring her to, even Asia. Hawaii would be more doable,

and we haven't yet been to the southeastern part of the States or even eastern Canada to see the ocean on that side.

I just want to travel the world with her.

In 2018, I got a job offer up north to work on a reserve, so that summer before my job started, I decided to road-trip all the way to Victoria Island, Canada. It was our first time camping together, just Kaia and I, and we camped the whole way. I think our bond really strengthened then. Her recall solidified during that trip—she knew to come back to me.

She had so much fun in Vancouver, because there are dog beaches. It was her first time touching the ocean, then licking the ocean water, and then realizing it wasn't good. On one of our hikes, it was super muddy. The mud was up to her shoulders at one point, and this tiny corgi was like, "This is the best thing ever!" She looked like a pig before we washed her off in the ocean.

Certain things are challenging with a corgi, for sure—like when there's mud up to their shoulders. Mostly, it's the river crossings. When dog owners talk about a trail, they'll say, "The river is shallow. Your dog can walk right over it." Well, that's generally not true for a corgi. She's pretty good at finding rocks to jump over, but a lot of the time I'll have to carry her. Big boulders can be a challenge as well; we were recently in the Yukon Territory, where there are a bunch of boulder fields. A lot of people warned me not to go, but she did fine. She could pick out her steps pretty easily.

A lot of people automatically think, *Oh, your corgi can't do that*. But I think so long as you're prepared, just like with any other dog, they'll be okay. After all, corgis were bred to run all day.

Corgis are pretty underestimated as adventure dogs.

—*@whereskaia*

If she were a human, she'd be very introverted but very adventurous.

WINTER

WINTER WEATHER brings unique adventures. With snowfall comes new ways to play: skiing, snowshoeing, (safely) exploring frozen places, and more. There's car camping and sleeping-bag snuggles, and extra wood on the fire to keep warm—plus some irresistibly cute doggo gear to help our fur friends stay comfortable in low temps (ahem, parkas and ski goggles!). Whether they're backcountry skiing, braving a snowmobile ride, or just getting cozy by the campfire, some pups just can't wait for winter!

BELOW: Chewie in fluffy marshmallow snow at Twin Lakes Resort in Bridgeport, California.

OPPOSITE: After a five-mile snowmobile ride, Kicker stands at camp just outside the Wyoming High Country Lodge.

MOGLI, SUMMIT, SIMON & KATHA

Adventurers in the Swiss Alps strengthen their bond with every hike.

My husband Simon and I had never owned dogs before. Simon broke his leg climbing, and I thought he needed a companion while I was at work and studying. That's how the idea of getting a dog first came to us. We researched dog breeds that are good for outdoor activities, and the Australian shepherd was one of them. So then we researched more on dogs in general and Australian shepherds especially. Finally, we found a breeder who had puppies.

On their website, there was an adorable pup we arranged to meet. But when we got there, the breeder had other pups as well, and that's when we met Mogli—he wasn't the dog in the original picture. He was a bit shy, but then he became friends with my husband's crutches. He started chewing on them! And that's how he chose us.

We were enchanted. We loved him immediately.

We got Summit a year later from the same breeder, because we wanted a companion for Mogli. Mogli is rather reserved and very down-to-earth, so we thought we'd look for a pup who was opposite to him—one that's more lively and who can take Mogli out of his shell. We told the breeder all of that, and she found us Summit. He's exactly what we asked for!

ABOVE: A beautiful hike after a cold night in the camper. Good things those dogs never get cold!

OPPOSITE: Mogli and Summit posing in front of the biggest glacier in Europe.

Mogli in front of one of his backyard mountains.

If Mogli has the choice, he'd rather be outdoors.

to move to the mountains. Once we got Mogli, we knew it was time. Half a year later, we moved from Germany to the Swiss mountains.

We started adventuring on trails and exploring our surroundings with Mogli. It immediately clicked with him. If he has the choice, he'd rather be outdoors. He's a bit of a loner, so he runs off when he finds something more interesting, but mostly he stays with us. Summit had no choice but to join us on our adventures when he came along.

We've moved several times since we first arrived in Switzerland, always closer to the mountains. Now we can actually start mountain hikes from our doorstep. We love everything in the mountains—the waterfalls, mountain lakes, and mountaintops. We hope to take the dogs to the highest hiking summit here in Switzerland.

Mogli and Summit are really great together. Sometimes they have a little bit of beef, just like brothers might have, but at the end of the day, they love each other and it's going great.

When Simon and I met, we were living in the city, but we already knew we wanted

Our favorite moments with Mogli and Summit are when we can let them both off-leash (it's not always possible with Mogli). We love when we have a really great background and a huge meadow to let them run in, because they're having the time of their lives playing in such beautiful places. And of course, Simon and I get to take in the views.

Everything dogs learn when they're younger makes it easier for them when they're older. Try to get your dogs used to anything you might encounter while adventuring: skiers when you're hiking in winter; all kinds of wildlife; different surfaces, like suspension bridges. Mogli, for example, has a strong herding instinct, so he goes crazy when he sees skiers. Going into a ski area with him? No can do. If we'd known that when he was younger, we might have been able to help him get used to stuff like that. But he was our first dog, so we didn't know.

We don't have many dangerous animals here, luckily. There are a lot of marmots, and when Mogli hears them, he runs off because of his strong prey drive. Not my favorite sound! We also have mountain goats, which are really magnificent. They keep their

A scene from one of the few times Mogli, Summit, Simon, and Katha went mountaineering, an unforgettable adventure.

distance. Sometimes in the mountains, along the tree line, we see deer.

But one time, Mogli was bitten by a snake right on the trail. I'd never seen a snake outdoors before. We were hiking up an incline, and he was sniffing in the bushes along the path. Suddenly, we saw the snake strike out and bite him on his snout. In no time, it was really swollen. We knew it must have been a venomous snake. We decided we needed to break off our hike and get down off the mountain, but unfortunately we were in the middle of nowhere. That's where Mogli proved to be

RIGHT: Summit at the summit. This dog definitely lives up to his name.

BELOW: Mogli and Summit in a glacier cave.

the best adventure buddy, because he made it his task to bring us down safely before he collapsed. When we reached the car, he was out of strength and tired.

We didn't even know there were venomous snakes in Switzerland until it happened. It was really scary because we didn't know what to do with him. We read that he needed to flush out the poison by drinking a lot of water, which he didn't do. It was almost like he was on drugs because he was totally not like himself. He wouldn't react to anything at all and just wanted to be left in peace.

Once he was recovered, he was fine. And it didn't even leave an impression. The next time we went out, he had his nose right back in the bushes. My husband always says it made him like Spider-Man after being bitten by the spider. Mogli is a superdog now. He never gets tired, and he's not scared of anything.

I work from home, so I'm with the dogs all the time. But Simon is at an office during the day, and the dogs have to say goodbye to their dog dad every morning. Mogli and Summit are really most content when all four of us are together and outdoors or in the van, making the most of it.

Adventuring with the dogs really helped us to improve our bonds with them. It's not that they are the best-behaved dogs—I wouldn't say that—but the bond between us gets stronger with every adventure. It's a reason to keep going further.

—@swiss.paws

The bond between us gets stronger with every adventure.

Happy times in the deep snow—the best way to get these dogs tired!

ENZO, LUCA, TESSA & MARTIN

Two "wild wolf boys" and their people make the mountains part of their story.

Enzo was a long time coming. We had lived abroad and then moved to San Francisco for work, and then finally we felt like we were in a place where we could support a dog. We started looking at local rescues, and as soon as we saw Enzo, Martin was in love—Enzo looked like a little lion cub. It was very competitive to adopt dogs in San Francisco at the

time—there were so many rescues that we never heard back from—but within minutes of receiving our email inquiring about Enzo, the rescue emailed back and we set up a time to meet at a park.

Enzo was four months old and it was love at first sight. We took him home that weekend, and from there it's been nonstop adventure. Immediately after Enzo was handed over to us, we put him in the car

and drove straight to the beach. It ended up being his favorite spot, and still is.

We decided we wanted him to live the best possible life, because he had been a stray. We took Enzo to the beach every day. Martin would go to work really early, so he could leave as early as possible at the end of the day, and I would go in as late as possible so I could get up at six to take Enzo to the beach before work. Martin would be home

ABOVE: Enzo in his element, enjoying a snowy hike up a mountain in Como, Colorado.

OPPOSITE: Enzo and Luca enjoying a game of wrestle in the fresh powder.

ABOVE: Martin proposing to Tessa at Fallen Leaf Lake while visiting Lake Tahoe, California.

OPPOSITE TOP: Enjoying a day on the lake—frozen lake, that is. Enzo on ice at Eleven Mile State Park in Colorado.

OPPOSITE BOTTOM: Partners in crime. Enzo and Luca exploring in the mountains together near Alma, Colorado.

around four to walk Enzo every night—and then it was back to the beach or to the dog park. It was work and Enzo. That's all we did for about a year.

We knew at the time we didn't love living in a city, but Enzo loves cities. We would bring him into downtown San Francisco on the weekends, and he just loved all the smells and the people and the scraps of food he could find—he never outgrew that strayness in him. We took him to all the sites: Pier 39, the cable cars on Hyde Street. When we weren't in the city, we would try to get out

and go camping. We went to Tahoe, Alabama Hills, Yosemite—everywhere in California that we could find that was fun.

It was an adventure-filled life from the start, but it also seemed like something was missing. Enzo loved all the dogs in our neighborhood (and had a weird affinity for corgis). He had his little crew of best friends at the dog park and loved playing. Then, about a month before Covid really hit, we thought, *We should get a second dog.*

Luca needed us, but more than us, he needed Enzo.

We lost out on so many dogs before we found Luca. We saw his picture at the Marin Humane Society website. He was such a little puppy, about three months old. In his photo, his ears were down and he looked so sad and scared. We called and asked if he was available, and they were kind of shocked that someone was interested in him. We brought Enzo with us when we went to meet him.

Poor Luca. We don't know what happened to him in his early stages of life, but he was such a traumatized little dog. He wasn't even

We learned that it's on us to look out for Enzo and set him up for success.

in the shelter with the rest of the dogs. The behavioral specialist had taken a liking to him, and Luca spent his shelter days in their office. It took a few minutes for Luca to come up to us. But Enzo immediately ran up to him. Luca was somewhat caught off guard by Enzo's boldness and barked in his face. Enzo kind of smiled at him (as much as a dog can smile), let Luca know that we were safe, and then they started playing. Luca followed Enzo everywhere, and they were immediate best buds. On the ride home, they were snuggled together in the car. We were expecting a little acclimation time, like Enzo might protect his toys. But that never happened. From the start, they were sharing bones, actually chewing on the same bone from opposite ends at the same time. They were instant best friends.

Luca needed us, but more than us, he needed Enzo. He needed a big brave dog to teach him how to be a dog. And Enzo definitely is that big brave dog.

Enzo is overwhelmed by nothing. Honestly, it's his biggest flaw: his lack of fear. While living in San Francisco, we had heard about this really great dog beach, so we went, but didn't realize that the dog section is elevated on a cliff with the beach below. We let Enzo off his leash in the off-leash area, but it wasn't really fenced. Everything was fine until Enzo saw some birds and just chased them straight off the cliff. He somehow got himself stuck halfway down

the cliff and there was no way for us to get to him. A huge crowd of people gathered on the beach below, and someone called the fire crew. Martin was running around trying to call Enzo from below on the beach, and I was waiting at the top. I went to find the firefighters that had come to save our dog—I even rode with them in the fire truck. But then Enzo suddenly decided, "I can get myself out of this situation." And he just went for it: He jumped up and clung to the top of the cliff with his front paws with the rest of his body dangerously dangling off the cliff, almost like a *Lion King* scene, and pulled himself up.

We learned that it's on us to look out for Enzo and set him up for success. If there's likely to be wildlife or something potentially hazardous on a trail, we keep him leashed.

We're always very, very alert, and we really check out a place or situation beforehand. He's gotten better too. I think he learned that if he wants freedom, he needs to respect some boundaries.

Luca was challenging in other ways. He's our big scaredy-cat baby. Where Enzo is strong-willed and confident, has no fear, and needs wrangling, Luca was the most obedient puppy. We never had to train him, and he listens really well. He just naturally stuck with us. But he is so scared of everything. The city was the worst thing for him. He hated being there. Nature, on the other hand—he loved!

Luca does great in the wild. He's still skittish around people, and he's a bit reactive with other dogs. Similar to how we had to learn to set up Enzo for success with wildlife,

ABOVE: A quick game of chase on a frozen Apline lake on Guanella Pass, Colorado.

OPPOSITE TOP: Catch me if you can! Enzo and Luca racing each other at Eleven Mile State Park, Colorado.

OPPOSITE BOTTOM: Luca, the happy mountain mutt, cheesin' somewhere in Colorado.

ABOVE: Enzo, the self-proclaimed king of the mountain, striking a pose at Square Top Lake, Colorado.

OPPOSITE: The "wild wolf boys," adventuring together near Breckenridge, Colorado.

we had to learn how to set up Luca for success so he could hike on crowded trails. Owners often claim that their dogs are "friendly," but most "friendly" dogs don't properly read Luca's body language and end up setting him off, ruining weeks or months of training. We're very much advocating for Luca on hikes and removing him from potentially bad situations.

We want to go everywhere with Enzo and Luca. Traveling with them is so much more appealing to us. I don't think any adventure is too big or too small; if all you can do is walk your dogs around the neighborhood or take them to a local park or something, that's where it starts. You don't need mountains and oceans and lakes to have an adventure; it's just important to be out there with your dog, showing them the world.

Ultimately, our favorite places to go are in the mountains. Mountains have always been a part of our story. We met hiking in the mountains, and when we just got Enzo, we went up to Tahoe for a weekend, where we went on a long hike to this alpine lake. We had Enzo's Instagram going, so it was standard for Martin to set up the tripod and say, "Let's get a cute picture together." We were sitting on a log by the lake and Enzo was in my lap. It was so beautiful. And that's when Martin proposed. We captured it perfectly on camera, and Enzo's right there. Enzo's always in the middle of everything.

We got married on a mountain too. We couldn't have a wedding at the time because of Covid, so we hiked to the top of a mountain with just Enzo and Luca and got married up there.

One of my favorite things about camping is in the evening, when we're sitting by the campfire. It's nice to see Enzo and Luca lying outside. I know they're very, very distant descendants of wolves, but wolves are out there in the wild sleeping and, when we're camping, so are Enzo and Luca. I just feel like they're so at peace. Enzo will build a little nest for himself and curl up in it, and he just looks like he belongs there.

—*@wildwolfboys*

MAKO & KAETLYNN

A husky and her human, at home in the big wide world.

For about as long as I knew, I didn't want kids, I've wanted a husky—which is funny, because I'm pretty sure my dog talks back more than a child does! I had finally gotten to a point in my life where I had a backyard, and I was ready to get a dog. I had been looking for a long time with a bunch of husky rescues in Arizona. I took the weekend to think

about one dog, and when I called back, she'd already been adopted. But it was serendipity—it's because she wasn't the one that was supposed to be. I eventually saw this post on Lucky Huskies rescue about an eleven-month-old dog, which was younger than what I wanted—I did not want to go through the puppy stage. But once I saw her, I completely fell in love. I thought, *I need her in my life.*

I named her Mako, which is a type of shark. They're the fastest shark in the sea, and it turns out, so is my Mako! She's like thirty-five or forty pounds—a mini husky—very small, but super speedy. She is obsessed with food. She will just shark it right out of your hands if you're not paying attention.

She's super goofy. Her tongue sticks out one inch at all times. I can be so upset about something, and then I look over and her

ABOVE: Mako takes in the sunset at her and Kaetlynn's favorite sand dunes.

OPPOSITE: Summit snuggles on the top of Browns Peak in Arizona.

ABOVE: Lava tube
light magic.

OPPOSITE: Mako
relaxes in the hammock
after backpacking.

tongue is out and I just start laughing. You
can make her tongue come out like a Pez
dispenser if you hold her nose and shake it
a little bit. There's nothing that makes me
happier than my dog's tongue.

She's also a lover. She loves to snuggle,
she loves to play, and she's great with kids
and older folks. She's just a very loving,
squishy, goofy dog. But she is also *a lot*.
She is a *husky*. If you don't like dogs, you
probably won't like my dog because she is a
real dog-person's dog. She likes to run after

bunnies and steal food from counters and
chases her tail and jumps on you when she's
excited. She has her own personality.

Mako took to the outdoors really quickly. She
just likes to be outside as much as I do, so I feel
really blessed. She's a great hiker; she's got great
stamina, tough paws. She loves to paddleboard
and kayak—I think because she knows I like
the water so much. She loves camping. She's a
great little backpacker. She carries my booze

when we go camping and hiking—just to clarify, that's because water weight is the easiest to balance! So she carries my beers and I carry all her food. That's our deal.

My favorite Mako-ism is that, when we're home, she is the bougiest bitch. She sleeps on my bed and totally sprawls out. But when we camp, I'll put a blanket down for her in the tent, and she just kicks it away and goes to the farthest corner possible and makes a point to sleep directly on the ground. She looks at me like, "I'm a wolf. I'm in the wild. I don't need bedding or the trappings of society!"

Mako and I live in a converted school bus. We usually live in Arizona and would consider that our home now. But when I built the school bus, I drove it up to Washington State, where my folks are from. We were busy building most weeknights and most weekends, so I didn't get to give Mako as much love and attention as I usually do. But we were right down the street from a mountain. So early on Saturday or Sunday mornings, I would prioritize her. We would hike Mount Erie, and Mako got to be off-leash because nobody was out there as early as we were. We would climb all the way to the top and we'd sit and look at the beautiful view. I try to give her as many opportunities as possible to just be a dog—off-leash, exploring, stopping to smell the roses.

I thought, *I need her in my life.*

Mako has made me a better dog owner.

It was a lot of work to build the bus, as well as to live voluntarily with my parents in my thirties in the middle of a pandemic. So those hikes with my furry best friend were really some of what saved me that year, emotionally and physically.

I still do a lot of work with the rescue where I got Mako, especially in husky education. Huskies are not for everyone; all breeds are trainable, but huskies are definitely for people who are active—they are such good running partners and hiking partners. But you always have to be aware of breed tendencies. Huskies are prey driven. They're independent animals. You have to accept the fact that that dog might need to be on a leash a lot.

Sometimes I think that maybe in the future, it'd be nice to have a dog I don't always have to have on a leash. But Mako has made me a better dog owner. It took me a lot of trial and error. If I had a dog that was easily able to be off-leash and had good recall from the start, I think I wouldn't be so conscious of the environment and what's good for them and what's good for other animals.

A lot of people got huskies because of *Game of Thrones*, but they didn't realize how much work they are. For example, in Arizona in the summer, people can't exercise their dogs as much because it's so hot, and then their husky eats their couch and they abandon their dog. We see an uptick of abandonment of huskies in the summer.

If you're ready for an adventure dog, do your research. Wait for the right match. Make sure that it's going to be a good lifestyle fit for you, or that it's going to encourage you to level up your lifestyle.

I definitely get outside more because of my dog. I've always been active, but on days that I do not want to get out of bed, I do because of my dog. I feel like every dog owner can say that: On the days that you are just like, *I can't do this, I don't want to do this, I don't want to be here, I don't want to be active*—whatever the situation—Mako helps me get out, and I always feel better when I'm outside.

I've fostered about ten different dogs through Lucky Huskies now. They've been everywhere from several-week-old puppies to five- or six-year-old dogs. It's funny, when I foster, everyone's always like, "You have to keep them!" But I just have never felt the same way about a dog as I do about Mako.

Mako and I have a very good relationship. One day maybe I'll add a dog to the pack. But she and I have a really good thing going right now, and I love that it's just the two of us. And we live in a bus, so I literally cannot fit another dog. The dog would have to be a chihuahua. It's not happening!

But when we're in the bus, out in the desert in East Phoenix, we hear the coyotes howl. Mako and I will sit outside and just listen to them. For her, it's like her people. It's magical for both of us because coyotes are so incredible, and the desert is so beautiful.

In moments like that, your dog is not just a dog but this being that is in tune with the universe like you are. It's little moments like that that make me fall in love with her again and again.

—*@girlandhusky*

ABOVE: Being cute for trail treats!

OPPOSITE: Mako and Kaetlynn explore lava tubes in the desert.

BOOTER, KICKER & ANDREW

After a tragic loss, a puppy has some big paws to fill. And he does.

My first dog, Booter, and I were wrapping up an epic six-month road trip, and on our way home I was driving a bit later than I should have been. I should have pulled over when I got tired, but instead I tried to keep pushing and we got into a horrible car accident, and I lost Booter. After the crash, I was on the side of the road, just sobbing and wanting to get run over by a car, honestly. The paramedics were trying to chat me up about climbing and telling me about their previous adventures. All I could think was, *Leave me alone. I just lost everything.* But then a volunteer firefighter came up and put his arm around my shoulders and said, "Hey, man, I am so sorry. I don't know exactly what you're going through right now, but I can relate." He was just quietly there for me and helped me through one of the most challenging nights of my entire life.

I had filmed most of my adventures with Booter over the course of our trip and had a bunch of cool footage. I told the volunteer firefighter, "I want to share with you how special Booter was and how special our bond was." So I got his information to send him some videos, and we stayed in contact for about two months.

ABOVE: Booter and Andrew hiked up Mt. Hood in Oregon to catch the sunset before skiing down.

OPPOSITE: Kicker and Andrew ventured out to the Fifth Water Hot Springs in the winter. Of course, Kicker had to pose for a photo.

RIGHT: Booter under the stars.

BELOW: Kicker enjoying the view of Mt. Hood from the across the Columbia River Gorge.

OPPOSITE TOP: Ski touring is Kicker's favorite activity.

OPPOSITE BOTTOM: Snow is definitely Kicker's favorite weather.

Randomly, he called me up one day and said, "I have an opportunity for you. But I want to share a story first." He went into how, when he was my age, he tragically lost the best dog he could have ever imagined—which was exactly like Booter to me—and how his parents got him another dog, even though he never felt like he'd be ready to love another one, and how much that helped him heal. He told me that he and his family bred goldens and goldendoodles, and that when I was ready they had one for me.

A few weeks later, the pieces of my life were coming back together in a way that I could

The more you can introduce a dog to, the more trust you can build.

see myself being able to give a dog the best life possible. So I went and checked out a litter of puppies at the firefighter's family home.

When I first picked out Booter, it was maybe three minutes before I said, "That's my dog. That's the one." But this was way harder. All the puppies were so cute and so similar and all had great personalities, even at five weeks old. I spent about five hours there trying to decide. I don't think they quite expected me to hang out that long in their house. They were like, "Okay, we need to eat dinner—would you like to join?" It was a huge decision, though.

Eventually, Kicker and I connected. He was hanging out in my lap, and then he fell asleep. He was definitely more drawn to me than the other puppies—he just wanted to be around me. So I thought, *Okay, this is the one.*

After having the dog of my dreams— a dog better than I could have ever imagined—I wasn't sure I could be so fortunate to get another dog even close to that. Kicker has just been absolutely incredible. I've had two of the best dogs that anybody could ever ask for, and I am so grateful.

With Booter, it was a progression into that lifestyle. He was my first dog, and I was kind of young when I got him. I was working at a park where I could bring him with me, but I was pretty focused on the job. Now I'm working full-time as an adventurer and content creator. So Kicker was kind of thrown into the lifestyle. I was living in a van when I got him, and then a month later, we drove up to Alaska for three months. For Kicker, it was just immediate—he was in my jacket snowboarding with me, he was kiteboarding with me, he was doing all these crazy things just in my jacket or in my pack. Then as he grew stronger, he would run for a little bit and then I'd carry him. Eventually he got to the point where he could hold his own. Kicker just

ABOVE: Kicker rocking the latest Velcro blanket fashion.

RIGHT: When Kicker was just a pup, he and Andrew made a dream trip come true and drove to Alaska. This is from the first moment in Haines, Alaska.

Being in the woods, going on adventures, being in nature—that's who I am and how I've always been. Before I got a dog, I imagined this lifestyle and always pictured a dog off-leash by my side backpacking and camping. My thought was that if I introduced a dog to everything early and often, and kept them happy and safe along the way, they'd understand that that's our way of life.

showed up and was like, *All right, this is cool. This is life. We're doing it.*

Introducing dogs to things early and often and staying well within your skill set so that the dog is happy and feels safe is just so important. I really focus on that when raising my dogs. Nothing I do will compromise my safety or my dog's.

The more you can introduce a dog to, the more trust you can build. There have been times where we're doing something and I've had to carry Kicker down a steep incline or whatever and he looks at me like, "I'm not so sure about this." The more you encounter those things and you're able to safely execute, the more trust the dog builds and the more confident they are in your ability.

Prioritizing your dog's safety is always the most important thing—if they get hurt, then you lose that trust.

Kicker and I have been fortunate enough to travel all over the place. We've been up to Alaska and all the way down to Baja. My bucket list is just to continue to be able to bring Kicker everywhere, as much as I possibly can.

Our favorite place is probably a spot called Thompson Pass, which is in these big, glacial Alaska mountains. That's really where Kicker and I got to meet each other and grow and spend time. We went when he was a puppy, and we went back six years later, in spring. Every time we go, it's so special. This past spring, people

Kicker is a lover of all. He doesn't chase deer, elk, or moose, and he even welcomes three-legged cat friends.

he just calmly looks over, like he's thinking, *The deer's doing his thing. I'm doing my thing.* Kicker doesn't want to chase it.

One afternoon, there was a whole herd of elk basically in our backyard. I spent four or five hours shooting photos of the elk, with Kicker just hanging out by my side. At first, I had him way far back, away from the elk. But eventually, he was lying in the snow next to me, with two massive bull elk fifty feet away from him—and he wasn't even looking at them. I've never seen a dog so chill. He just wants everyone to be happy and wants to be friends with everybody—he's not trying to cause a ruckus.

We spend so much time outside in the woods and on the trail that he's like, *This is how I live.* He enjoys smelling things and peeing on things and being a dog, but none of that is a novelty for him because he's had so much of it. I'm a huge believer in letting dogs be dogs when you can. So if we're in a place that's safe and not too many people are around, I just let him go and smell and bring sticks and be a dog.

ABOVE: On set for the short film *Companions*, a ski film about dogs, for which Andrew and Kicker lived in a backcountry cabin for ten days.

OPPOSITE TOP: Booter rests after spending the night keeping Andrew company while he shot photos of the Milky Way.

OPPOSITE BOTTOM: Kicker on the *Companions* set after summiting the best ski line of the trip. He is really in his element!

there saw us and said, "Oh my god, it's Kicker! He's so big!" Six years later, everyone remembers this random dog that they met once. It's such an adventure spot, and Kicker just seems to thrive there. He loves the snow and loves camping, and the combination of those two for an extended period of time is his favorite.

Kicker is super funny when it comes to wildlife. He just doesn't care. I'll nudge him all excitedly and say, "Look, there's a deer!" But

I love my dogs with every fiber of my being. At first I was nervous that I would hold Kicker to the same standard as Booter. Booter and I had five years to develop that relationship where I could look at him and he could look at me, and I would know what he needed from me and he knew what I wanted from him.

Prioritizing your dog's safety is always the most important thing.

It took me a little while with Kicker to realize that this puppy didn't even know his name, much less what I expected from him. It took some active cognitive thought on my part: *It's a puppy. You can't expect this to be Booter.* Those shoes aren't fillable—Booter was irreplaceable. But Kicker totally rose to the occasion and did ultimately fill some incredibly big shoes and hole in my heart. And Kicker and I can speak to each other with our eyes at this point.

There are subtle differences between Booter and Kicker. Kicker is definitely a smellier dog and a bit more snuggly. But their personalities and their trust in me and their willingness to go on all these wild adventures are almost indistinguishable. They both have the same "Okay, we're doing this! I trust you!" attitude. I love them and respect them equally. They're both exceptional dogs, and I'm super fortunate.

There's still sadness in the loss of Booter—it will always make me sad to think about. But I definitely love Kicker just as much, if not more, in the light of that loss.

—*@kickerdogmuse and @andrew__muse*

PE'AHI, NALU, LEILANI, HONU & ALTA

A pack of rescued cattle dogs and their people explore Alaska.

I got my first dog, Pe'ahi, in 2004. I'm a runner, and I wanted a dog that could keep up with me. And I wanted a dog that was unique in coloring—not an all-black or all-brown dog. I came across a bunch of cattle dog mixes online. Pe'ahi ended up being one of two remaining in a litter of eleven. I actually went to meet his brother, but when we got there, we fell in love

with him. Pe'ahi was sitting perfectly quietly in a kennel while everybody else was barking and going crazy. So I said, "Yeah, that one. He looks mellow."

The day they brought him home to us, he ran figure eights in the backyard for forty-five minutes straight. And I thought, *I chose the wrong dog.* I had a

total panic attack because I didn't know what I was doing or what I was getting myself into.

But then I took him for the first walk. I asked him, "Hey, do you want to be my running partner?" and when I said "run," he did. And I thought, *All right. I guess you're kind of cool. We'll make this work.*

ABOVE: The crew photographed on one of their favorite local islands to camp on in Juneau, Alaska.

OPPOSITE: One of the last outings as a family before Pe'ahi passed.

Nalu is my soul.

I was having a really hard time thinking of a name that fit him and finally turned to an atlas for ideas when my partner at the time, who was a surfer, suggested Pe'ahi. It's the name of a big wave surf spot in Maui that surfers also call "Jaws." Pe'ahi was very mouthy as a puppy, so it fit perfectly.

Pe'ahi was my main dude—my only dude—for eight years. He ran with me six days a week for seven years. Then I thought he was getting arthritis, but it turned out he had blown a cruciate. He was eight when he had knee surgery and stopped running completely.

Around that time, I had started thinking about getting a second dog. I was looking at fostering a bull terrier, but at a barbecue, a friend told me her brother's next-door neighbor had a litter. Then she showed me

a picture of this puppy. He was ridiculously adorable, because cattle dog puppies are probably the cutest things on the planet. So I said, "Yeah! That one! I'll take him."

That's Nalu. Pe'ahi was my first dog ever as my own, so he obviously will forever hold a special place. But Nalu is my soul. When naming him, I decided to stick with the theme I started with naming Pe'ahi. Nalu means "ocean" or "wave" in Hawaiian, because these have always been calming elements for me. And Nalu is my source of calm, my go-to happy place in times of stress.

After I got Nalu, I found out that the people who owned his parents were not particularly responsible dog owners. Not bad people by any means, but they just had very different cultural standards on what you do with dogs. They had two intact adults who lived in a backyard together, and basically, every time the female went into heat, she got pregnant and had a litter.

At the time, I was involved with cattle dog rescue and had feelers in that world as far as placing puppies. So when the dogs had the next couple of litters, my friend's brother would reach out to me.

I ended up agreeing to foster the two females left in the next litter until a rescue could find homes for them. But when we went to pick them up, it took us forty-five minutes just to get Leilani

out of the house and into the car. She was about four months and just had no socialization at all. The sister was a bit more well-balanced and had a more even temperament. But Leilani hid under our table for a week, and she was terrified of everything. I realized that I wasn't comfortable giving this dog to just anyone. I had planned to adopt her out, but she grew on me and I realized I wanted to watch her grow.

The name Leilani means "heavenly blossom," and I can genuinely say it's been an honor to watch her blossom into the dog she is today.

ABOVE: Walking to the Mendenhall Glacier in Juneau when the lake freezes is one of Alta's favorite things to do.

OPPOSITE: On Boy Scout Beach, about a twenty-five-mile drive "out the road," as they say in Juneau. At low tide, the beach stretches for miles and offers stunning views of the Chilkat Range.

There was one final litter before we were able to get the owners to spay the female. And again, there were two females left. I didn't have homes lined up for those two—I thought I would just go get them and then figure it out. One of those was Honu, who is my youngest. We had her for a day and she was just not thriving. She was really lethargic; she wouldn't eat or drink. She was the size of a potato—just so small. I took her to the vet and she had pretty severe giardia and parvo. Thankfully, we caught it early so they treated her. The Instagram community helped contribute to her vet bills. But she was $1800 right out the gate. I thought, *Well, I guess I'm keeping this one too.* Honu is the

stereotypical little sister who just has to be in everybody's face. She starts everything, and then gets in trouble and wonders why she's in trouble. She's eight years old now and still acts like she's eight days old. She's the dog that will never grow up.

Honu means "turtle," which are signs of wisdom and good luck. Honu went through so much at the beginning of her life—I felt she was wise beyond her years and had certainly been lucky!

That's how I wound up with four dogs. Nalu, Leilani, and Honu are full siblings. They are currently ten, nine, and eight. It's been really amazing to watch how the siblings interact; their bond is so strong. I don't know

BELOW: A memory from their first summer in Juneau.

OPPOSITE: Another trip to Boy Scout Beach, with the snow-covered Chilkats stealing the show in the background.

Dredge Lakes is a favorite local trail.

I was not a hiker before I had dogs.

if dogs know they are related, but it sure seems like these guys do! Pe'ahi, my big man, passed in 2020. He was fifteen and a half. We miss him, every single day.

I was not a hiker before I had dogs. We were outdoorsy growing up, but we didn't really camp or do a lot of hiking. When I got Pe'ahi, I realized that he had to walk more than once a day—and I hated walking. If I was going somewhere, I was running. If I wasn't running, I was driving. But I realized that you can't run a dog three times a day. Pe'ahi got me into hiking because I didn't just want to walk around the neighborhood.

Pe'ahi had his knee surgery when he was eight, and we moved from Santa Cruz to Bend, Oregon, where we had a lot more opportunities to be outdoors with the dogs. Pe'ahi summitted South Sister, which is the third-tallest peak in Oregon, twice after his knee surgery. It's less than a twelve-mile round trip hike, but it's good elevation gain. That was a special moment for all of us. He was a champ.

Now we're in Alaska, and we get to do the things we want to be able to do with the dogs. They're almost always off-leash. Here, if you want to go camping, you drive down the road and find an empty spot and camp. Or you get on your boat and you go to an island and you're the only person on the island and you camp.

We live in Juneau—and when you're in Juneau, you're in Juneau. It's pretty isolated— only accessible by boat or air—and it's pretty far southeast. We have almost the entire state we haven't touched. We're really looking forward to getting up north in Alaska and doing some hiking, road-tripping, and camping.

When I first started adventuring with the dogs, I think I was really naïve. I had the mentality: *You want to do it? Go do that!* But

I look back on some of the things I've done with them and I think, *That was dumb. Probably shouldn't have done that.*

For people just starting out, I think the biggest thing is to not let all of the what-ifs stop you. Get out and do what you're comfortable with, and don't focus on all the minutiae to the point where you feel stuck and overwhelmed.

Also, know your dog. If you don't spend a lot of quality time with your dogs, you don't know what signs to look for. I'm with my dogs so often that I know all their triggers. I know when the girls' ears turn up, I have to start looking.

Research the breed you're getting and make sure you understand what their needs are. When I first rescued Pe'ahi, the rescue organization made sure that I did my research and knew what I was getting into, because cattle dogs are not always super social and they can be destructive if you're not providing them with what they need. For some people, that's agility or mental stimulation or teaching a bunch of tricks because they are super intelligent dogs. For me, that's hiking and exploring and watching them navigate difficult terrain because that's what I also enjoy doing. If you want a cattle dog, make sure they will really fit your lifestyle—because not everyone wants to walk dogs twelve miles a day in the rain and the snow and the wind.

People will ask me how my dogs are so good. I really give a lot of that credit to Pe'ahi. I didn't really trust him off-leash until he was two. But Pe'ahi was eight by the time we got Nalu, and by then Pe'ahi was just so dialed in on everything. Nalu was so infatuated with Pe'ahi that he basically said, "I'll do whatever you do!" And then the rest of the dogs just followed suit: Leilani wanted to be with Nalu, and then I got Honu, who only wanted to be with the rest of them.

I think a lot of it is routine too. We are out all day, every day. We hike or walk ten to twelve miles a day just on local trails around our neighborhood. So there's a lot of practice. But I think it's also their pack mentality. At least for me, I got lucky that way—they all kind of just wanted to be together.

—*@nalu.co*

The dogs got a lot of compliments on their snazzy outer attire on this trek out to the Mendenhall Glacier.

CHEWIE, KANDIE & MARK

It's nothing but bluebird days for a pair of goldendoodles and their owner.

I was looking tirelessly for a goldendoodle. They were pretty popular then—not as popular as they are now, but pretty close—and I couldn't find one. There were long waitlists, and I was even looking out of state. I was almost going to give up. But then I came across a listing from a breeder and it just worked out. They had one more boy and one more girl, and I just

ABOVE: Chewie and Kandie at Lower Twin Lakes in Bridgeport, California.

OPPOSITE: Chewie at the Whitney Portal Trailhead, California.

immediately loved the boy. He looked great—he had, and still has, these gorgeous highlights around his eyes. He's a straight coat goldendoodle, which is quite unique, and he's super fluffy.

Chewie was ten weeks old when we got him. I really lucked out that I found him; I think it was just meant to be.

We found Kandie through a breeder that utilizes Chewie's stud service. I knew that

Chewie and Kandie would be boyfriend and girlfriend, get married, honeymoon, and have puppies.

Chewie is a big floofball. He's ultra-friendly. A real gentle giant. He always has a ball in his mouth. He listens to me anyway, but if I have a ball, whatever I want him to do is guaranteed to happen. He's a therapy dog, so he does really well around other people. He was attacked by a husky when he was little, so he kind of puts out his chest around other fluffy dogs like huskies or shepherds. But I believe you're never done with training, so I have a trainer that helps us from time to time.

Kandie is just happy-go-lucky. She's a sweetheart. She's always by my side, but sometimes she roams off a little ahead and does her own thing. She can be a little spacy, maybe a little airheaded, but she's super loyal. They both love to lean against me and get a pet.

Chewie and Kandie on a short hike at Virgina Lakes to Red Lake, Eastern Sierra, California.

I believe you're never done with training.

I've always been an out-and-about type guy. A really good friend of mine owns cabins and a camping resort up in Bridgeport, California, called Twin Lakes Resort. That's what sparked us to be adventurous and to go to some really cool, picturesque places—being at Twin Lakes Resort and stopping at other places on the way.

We spend a lot of time up there. It's gorgeous. It's really busy when there are people there in the summer, so we go off-season, when we're pretty much the only ones there. We get the run of the whole place, and the dogs get to do whatever and run wherever they want.

We love the cold weather—the more snow, the better. We like to go when there are feet coming down and it's dumping. We like to open the door in the morning on a bluebird day and get out there. The dogs love the ice and snow. Chewie doesn't care what the temperature is or what's going on: He'll always go in the water or out on the ice. Kandie's a little more dainty; she loves playing in the snow, but she's more hesitant about the water. We all love playing on the ice and, when it's safe, going out on frozen lakes.

My favorite memory to date is at Virginia Lakes. It was nice weather; there was snow

everywhere. The lake was still super frozen over. People had hiked to the top of the nearby peak and were skiing down it, and the dogs were staring at the skiers. They looked like they were thinking, *What's that? Are they aliens coming down or . . . ?* There are so many memories—every time we go somewhere, there's a great memory—but that one sticks out.

When we hit the road, we focus on the Eastern Sierras, and we specialize in travel up Highway 395. There are hundreds of lakes to stop at. Now I have a custom-made overland vehicle with a trailer and tent, so we can actually camp and post up next to alpine lakes.

We travel a lot locally too. There's a mountain that's close. We're about twenty minutes from the ocean. Cleveland National Forest is about thirty minutes away. When I was younger, I could basically snowboard and surf in the same day. We do that now too: We go to the mountains and we go to the beach.

Chewie and Kandie love the ocean and running on the sand. Chewie is so big in floof factor, but if he has water on him he just deflates into a lean stud.

When you're adventuring with your dogs, you always need to be aware of your surroundings. Where we go there are mountain lions, bears,

Chewie looking up at Mount Whitney in California.

rattlesnakes, bobcats, and more. There are animals that could jeopardize our dogs' lives and ours, so you have to be aware. And you need the right equipment for where you're going. Plan ahead—jackets for the humans, sweaters for the dogs, life preservers, paw wax when it's cold, plenty of food, water for the dogs, and of course a first aid kit for humans and dogs.

Be sensitive with where you go too. Here, it's so hot that we have to go where there's altitude. Goldendoodles, and especially Chewie, are looking for shade all the time. (Chewie has "shadar"—he's always looking

We love the cold weather—the more snow, the better.

ABOVE: Kandie loves to play in (and eat) the snow. Here, she's at Twin Lakes Resort in Bridgeport.

OPPOSITE: Chewie is always looking for a photo, pictured here in Holcomb Valley, California.

for a shade tree.) So we're conscious of where we go—somewhere no hotter than eighty degrees, hopefully closer to seventy, and there has to be plenty of water wherever we stay.

When puppies are here, I sleep next to Kandie and the puppies for the first five weeks. At about week six, they graduate to the downstairs play palace and I am generally able to jump back into my bed. But I'm always hands-on doing different tests with the puppies, writing down notes for their temperaments, and doing different neurological exercises—I'm trying to set them up for success. I'm in a kind of Covid-style lockdown for at least eight weeks with them.

I enjoy my time with the puppies. I get semi-emotional when they all go home—they're like little kids going away to college or getting married. But once they're all with their families, we're busting at the seams, ready to get out of here for a little bit while we can.

The dogs know when we're going to hit the road because we usually get up at three or four in the morning. Kandie is always up at four or five, following me around. But Chewie is not a morning guy. Yet he knows when we're going somewhere; he can sense we're doing something and sees me pack up his Alpha Pak gear and his toys, and he's up.

We're excited to get back out on the road. I have to adventure in spurts. I'd love to live that lifestyle year-round, but there are other responsibilities, with my wife and children and the puppies, so I can't always disappear. But I try to take one or two of my kids when we do go, and we just enjoy our time.

We go to locations where a lot of people aren't. Life is just easier that way—a little more free.

—@trailhawkdoods and @sweetsdoodles

Kopa modeling out at Bonneville Salt Flats in Utah, which is a great location to visit for some cool photos!

RESOURCES

GETTING STARTED

A beginner's guide from sidewalk to summit.

Inspired to adventure with your dog beyond your neighborhood walks? Here are some tips for going farther afield—safely.

Make your dog's safety a priority. This is the first rule of any adventure with your dog: Your pup depends on you to put their safety above all else. It's an honor and a responsibility, so take it seriously. At the very minimum, always make sure you have enough water and food, research temperature considerations, and bring safety gear.

Just get out. You might think your dog is a wild animal, but if your time outdoors with them is limited to walks around the block before and after work, your pup might need more time to get used to everything outside. Challenge yourselves to spend more time just being out: an hour hanging in the backyard, a full afternoon at

the park with friends, a morning at the beach off-season. Being outdoors more will help expose your dog to all the stimuli nature can send your way—from birds to squirrels to smells to other dogs (and beyond!).

Take it slow. Of course, a human can't go from couch potato to climbing K2 without lots of training—and neither can your dog, even if they seem to have boundless energy. Start with longer walks to build up endurance, then move to short, easy hikes, and continue to increase these slowly and safely. Make observations and adjustments as you go to build those adventure muscles!

Do your research. You might be surprised about the places your dog can and can't go. National and state parks often allow four-legged friends only in certain areas (if they allow

them at all). Set yourself up for success by researching where you hope to go before you get there. (See page 192 for more on what to think about before you head off on an adventure.)

Practice makes pretty good! As more than one interviewee in this book mentioned, give yourself the chance to fail safely. Forgetting an essential item when you're car camping at a nearby park is much easier to deal with than when you're miles away on a huge expedition. The more you and your dog get out, the more you'll both know what you need and how to navigate trails, handle obstacles, and enjoy yourselves.

Have fun. Remember to laugh and learn when things don't work out the way you thought they would, and to savor the unexpectedly wonderful moments of adventuring with your best friend.

PLANNING AHEAD

Questions to answer before you adventure.

While you can't predict every scenario you might encounter on an adventure, it can help to brainstorm potential problems and make a loose plan to handle them. To start, think through the following questions:

- When was your last vet visit? Make sure your dog is well enough to adventure with you and that they're current on all their shots.
- Is your dog's collar and ID current? This is crucial should they be separated from you.
- Is the place you want to go dog-friendly? What are the leash laws? Are there bark ordinances or other constraints to be prepared for?
- How much water do you need to bring to keep yourself and your dog healthy and safe on your adventure? (The American Hiking Society recommends bringing at least eight ounces of water for each dog for every hour you'll be hiking.)
- What's the weather forecast? Hot and cold weather both have risks: Dogs can overheat and dehydrate easily, showing few or no signs before they're in serious trouble, and hypothermia and frostbite are concerns in winter months. Rain and thunderstorms pose their own problems. (See below for seasonal safety tips.)
- What's your route? Understand the terrain you'll be on and think about what that means for you and your dog, including any bodies of water, inclines, thick underbrush, etc.
- What animals share the space you'll be in? Do you need to think about venomous or poisonous animals? What about large predators? Small pests like ticks and mosquitoes? What do you need to carry with you to be prepared if you encounter them (e.g., bear spray, tick treatments)?
- Do you have the safety essentials? Make sure you replenish any first-aid supplies previously used. (See page 195 for a suggested packing list.)
- Do you need special gear for your trip, and is it in good shape? Make sure leashes and harnesses aren't fraying, sleeping bags and mats are free of tears, and that zippers function, etc.

SAFETY BASICS

YEAR-ROUND

No matter what time of year you're adventuring, always think about these safety issues:

- Make sure someone knows where you are. Tell someone who is not going with you where you'll be and when you will be back, and/or check in with them during your trip.
- Be aware of the weather. Temperatures are extremely important to think about when you're out with your dog. While exact recommendations vary depending on breed, age, and size of your dog, most experts recommend limiting outdoor time when the temperature is above eighty or below thirty-two degrees Fahrenheit. Also be aware of

rain, snow, and wind, and how that affects the terrain you are adventuring on and the conditions you are sleeping in.

- Hydration, hydration, hydration. Dehydration can occur in any season and any situation, so make sure you always have water on hand. It can be hard to tell when a dog needs water, too, so proactively take breaks.

- Don't forget car safety on your adventures. Make your dog as safe as possible by researching the best safety options for your pup and your car. Consider dog harness seat belts, zipline harnesses, crates, dog guards, or backseat barriers. Also be careful with windows—make sure they can't jump out and that the wind or other projectiles can't harm them.

SPRING

- Be ready for rainy days. Tote along some rain gear to make sure you and your dog will be as comfortable as possible, should it rain. Make sure to heed any park guidance about wet conditions— flooding and slippery or unstable ground are just some of the concerns to think about. Also,

pay attention to the forecast and make sure to find safe shelter if lightning becomes an issue.

- Be aware of allergies. Yes, dogs suffer seasonal allergies too! Bring wipes when you're hiking to clean allergens from paws and coats, bathe them after big hikes, and talk to your vet if you see regular allergy symptoms, like sneezing or runny eyes.

SUMMER

- Be aware of the temperature. Most experts recommend limiting or avoiding time outside when temperatures reach eighty degrees Fahrenheit. Don't forget about humidity—high-humidity climates mean heatstroke can set in faster.

- Plan access to shade. Make sure wherever your adventuring has tree cover so your dog can take breaks out of the sun. Bring dog-safe sunscreen as well.

- Plan access to water. Hiking along rivers or lakes gives your dog the chance to take a dip and lower their body temperature. (Make sure they don't drink untreated water, though—it can make them sick.)

- Especially when hiking on paved trails or rock, make sure that the surface won't burn your dog's paws.

- Watch for snakes and other dangerous animals. Cold-blooded reptiles love the heat, and their interactions with hikers can increase as the weather gets warmer.

- As always, know your dog. Heat affects different breeds, ages, and temperaments differently.

- Know the signs of heatstroke and dehydration. Panting and drooling, fast heart rate, and vomiting (especially blood) all signal trouble, as do muscle tremors, acting disoriented, and unconsciousness.

FALL

- Beware of pests. Make sure you're current with your vet's recommended flea and tick treatments before you head out. But also check your dog (and yourself!) for ticks during and after hikes. Giving your dog a good brushing or a bath after can also minimize tick and flea problems.

- Watch your step. That foliage sure is beautiful, but fallen leaves can hide hazards like uneven terrain or even snakes.

- Don't get caught in the cold. Pay close attention to the weather during your planned adventure, and make sure to pack layers in case temperatures dip unexpectedly.

WINTER

- Dress warm. Just like you, your dog should dress in layers. Get them a dog sweater, and top that with a dog jacket to keep their body heat in.
- In very snowy or frozen terrain, think about whether your dog needs extra protection on her pads. Boots or wax can help keep them comfortable on tough terrain.

- Sleep warm. Try car or camper camping when it's very cold. Otherwise, make sure you and your dog both have high-quality sleeping bags and sleeping mats for cold nights. Snuggling up together can also help you both keep warm with body heat.
- Drink water. Hydration isn't only important during the heat. You and your pup should both sip water throughout the day, and take water breaks regularly.
- Keep hikes short. In cold weather, most dogs can hike for forty-

five minutes to an hour. When temperatures are below freezing, hike for twenty minutes max.
- As always, know your dog. Cold affects different breeds, ages, and temperaments differently.
- Know the signs of hypothermia. Shivering can be the first clue that your dog may be experiencing hypothermia. Sluggishness, rapid and then slow heart rate, big pupils, quick breaths followed by slower, shallow breaths, and depression are just some of the other signs. Seek vet attention right away.

NECESSARY AND NICE-TO-HAVE GEAR

Not sure what to pack? Start here.

NECESSARY

Don't leave home without . . .

- **A fully stocked first-aid kit.** While most injuries are often minor, you always want to be prepared if your pup needs help. Talk with your vet on what to bring, but at least make sure your first-aid kit is stocked with:
  - **Bandages:** Wrapping open scratches and scrapes can help prevent infection, and elastic bandages can help provide compression for muscle strains.

- **Tweezers:** Keep these on hand for removing ticks and pulling out thorns and other sticky things.
- **Saline:** Use this as an eye wash for bugs or debris that get into your dog's eyes.
- **Benadryl/diphenhydramine:** Having these medications on hand in case of an extreme allergic reaction to a plant or bug sting or other bites can save the day. Consult with your veterinarian for dosing.

- **Styptic pencil:** For bleeding cuts, nicks, and broken nails, try a styptic pencil to seal small wounds.
- Water bottles
- Extra food and water
- Collapsible bowls
- **Temperature-essential items:** Your dog must stay cool on warm days and warm on cold days. Think through what you need— whether that be cooling vests or insulated sleeping bags—to keep your dog safe.

SAMPLE CHECKLIST FOR PACKING FOR YOUR PUP

- ☐ Collar and ID tags
- ☐ Medication
- ☐ Leash
- ☐ Harness
- ☐ Dog first-aid kit
- ☐ Emergency carrying harness

- ☐ Water
- ☐ Food
- ☐ Extra water and food
- ☐ Food bowl (collapsible)
- ☐ Water bowl (collapsible)
- ☐ Treats

- ☐ Poop bags
- ☐ Blankets or dog sleeping bag
- ☐ Doggy backpack
- ☐ Toys
- ☐ Pet-safe insect repellent
- ☐ Stake (for leash or tether)

- ☐ Towels
- ☐ Clothing layers (if cold)
- ☐ Booties (if cold or on rough terrain)
- ☐ Safety light
- ☐ Cooling collar

NICE TO HAVE

- **Microfiber towels:** If your dog loves to jump in a lake, or if you're hiking during the winter, these superabsorbent lightweight towels can help you both dry off.
- **Dog backpack:** While it's not a necessity, your dog can pull some of their own weight with a sturdy backpack. Your pup's pack must fit properly, and you have to make sure its weight is appropriate for your dog's size. Check with your vet for your specific dog, but generally, dogs can safely carry ten percent of their weight. Make sure that the pack is waterproof and its straps are padded.
- **Clothes:** Bringing layers, like a sweater and a jacket, as well as protective footwear can help in certain conditions.
- **Bandana:** Bring some flair to the trails! Make sure you and your pup are in matching colors.
- **Leash coupler:** Two dogs in your pack? Try a leash coupler for tangle-free hiking.
- **Cooling collar:** Dogs can have a hard time cooling down. Cooling collars can help keep your pup comfortable in warm weather.

SOME OF OUR FAVORITE PLACES FOR YOUR BUCKET LIST

Need some travel inspiration? Here are just some of the Camping With Dogs team's favorite dog-friendly spots to visit.

US NATIONAL PARKS
Grand Teton National Park, Wyoming
Take a walk on the wild side at Grand Teton National Park! Hike through the lake trails to capture stunning waterside views all under the peaks of Grand Teton. Watch out for moose, deer, and even horses, which are allowed on the trails!

Grand Canyon National Park
Show your dog one of the most famous natural landmarks in the world! Although pets need to remain on a leash, your dog is allowed to roam on the South Rim of the canyon. Connected to the main visitor center, dogs are also permitted on the Greenway Trail. The Mather Campground, Desert View Campground, and Trailer Village are all dog-friendly lodging sites for you and your pup to stay.

Great Sand Dunes National Park
Explore the dunes, walk around Medano Creek, or take a hike

around Montville Nature Trail—or anywhere in the park, as long as your dog is leashed. If you plan to visit in late spring or summer, be aware that sand temperatures can reach up to 150 degrees Fahrenheit—be safe, and plan to walk trails in the morning or late evening to protect those paws!

Hot Springs National Park

Arkansas' beloved Hot Springs National Park should be on every dog-lover's bucket list. Dogs are permitted on all twenty-six miles of trails, most of which are under two miles in length. Located within the park are trails leading in and out of the downtown district. While pets are not allowed in the historic buildings, stroll around the sidewalks of Bathhouse Row or check out one of the dog-friendly restaurants nearby.

ROAD TRIP DESTINATIONS
Aspen, Colorado

Located in the heart of Colorado, Aspen is a great place to get outdoors and explore the Rocky Mountains with your pup. In the summer, dogs can ride the Aspen Mountain Gondola, which has breathtaking views. Don't miss

Colorado's famous Rio Grande Trail and Maroon Bells.

Portland, Oregon

It's no surprise that the Pacific Northwest holds some of the best hiking spots in the world. When it comes to hiking in Oregon, Portland's Forest Park and Columbia River Gorge are two must-see stops.

Big Sky, Montana

Just an hour's drive from Yellowstone National Park, Big Sky has pet-friendly trails for a great outdoor workout. Check out Gallatin National Forest's North Fork and Cinnamon Mountain Trail for beautiful views of southern Montana.

Ocean City, Maryland

If the mountains aren't so much your thing, check out the East Coast in Ocean City! Locals love to visit Ocean City Dog Playground, just a few blocks from the beach. Northside Park is also a hidden gem with easy access to the bay and pier.

INTERNATIONAL INSPIRATION
Alberta, Canada

Visit Banff National Park in Canada

to see the turquoise-colored waters! The Canadian Rockies are also home to some of the largest boulders, including Okotoks Erratic (Big Rock) near Jasper National Park.

Bern, Switzerland

Immerse yourself in Swiss culture by traveling to the capital city of Bern. Take a stroll through Old Town with your dog to see the stunning waters of the Aare River. The famous eight-hundred-year-old clock tower is also a must-see. Hike the trails of Gurten Mountain to see the snowy caps of the Swiss Alps.

Oulu, Finland

Oulu's rich history and modern culture make it a favorite destination for many international travelers. Check out the dog-friendly beaches and catch the sunset with your pup.

Nice, France

What's better than taking a trip to the French Riviera? Bringing your dog! Hike the foothills of southeastern France and explore dog-friendly beaches near the Mediterranean Sea. Bring your pup an hour north to Gorges du Cians for hillside views of the French countryside.

TENT CAMPING WITH DOGS

Avoid being dog tired with these tips.

Catching some zzzzzzs with your dog in a tent can be a little more challenging than sleeping at home. Here are some tried-and-true tips for a better night's sleep:

- Practice: Don't let the first time your dog steps foot in your tent be on the actual camping trip! Set your tent up in your home or in your backyard and hang out in it regularly. Treats help, too!

- Keep your dog comfy: If they're used to a dog bed (or *your* bed), pick up a sleeping mat just for your pup and bring some blankets for them to nest in. The more comfortable your dog is while sleeping, the less restless they'll be throughout the night.
- Make some room: Your dog will be much more comfortable and feel more secure if they're next to you at night, rather than in a crate or a car. Make

sure your tent is spacious enough for both of you.
- Tire them out: Hopefully after a day of hiking and adventuring, your dog will be more than ready for bed. But especially on the first night of camping, make sure they're dog tired.
- Bring your dog's equivalent of a teddy bear: A comfort item like a toy or blanket, or even a quick treat, can help your adventure companion feel less stressed.

SIT. STAY. SAY CHEESE.

Taking share-worthy shots of your dogs.

COMPOSING THE SHOT

If you took art class in grade school, you might remember the "Rule of Threes." This idea breaks an image down into thirds, both vertically and horizontally, forming a grid over the scene you want to capture. For landscapes, it's great to position your pup in one of the outer thirds. The result is aesthetically pleasing and captures your dog *and* your beautiful surroundings.

WORKING WITH YOUR MODEL

A more complicated approach might be getting your dog to pose for the perfect shot. As with everything when adventuring with dogs, a little training goes a long way. Practice these commands:

- Stay: Posing, of course, involves holding still. Your dog should be able to hold a stay even if you back up thirty feet.

- Place: Use this command to communicate to your dog that you want them to go to and stay on a specific spot. Be it a big boulder or sturdy log, saying "place" when their body touches where you want them to be, and reinforcing that with a treat, helps them know that this is the right spot.
- Look: Sometimes you just want to see those puppy dog eyes

staring straight into the camera. Teaching your dog "look"—to look directly at you—makes this much easier.

BE SNAP HAPPY

Even if they "stay" like a champ, dogs don't always stay still: They've got lolling tongues, blinking eyes, heads on a swivel. By taking twenty shots instead of two, you have a better chance of capturing pure gold. And thanks to digital, you can delete what you don't want later.

BENEFITS OF ADVENTURING WITH YOUR DOG

Camping With Dogs is on a mission to encourage dog owners to get outdoors with their pets. Here are just a few of the benefits you can experience when you adventure with your dog:

It's good physical activity. Outdoor adventuring like hiking and skiing raises your heart rate—and your dog's too. You'll both strengthen muscles and increase endurance by going out regularly. Breeds known for independence and high-energy dogs especially can be transformed by regular outdoor exercise.

It provides enrichment experiences for your dog. Dogs, like humans, need activities to keep them busy and maintain their active brains.

Although there are plenty of indoor enrichment activities for your dog, hiking or camping outside opens up their world. Dogs need to sniff, and scenting in nature—smelling plants and encountering animals—enlivens their experiences.

It will make you both happier. Lots of research has shown that getting outside improves humans' mental health, lowering anxiety and boosting spirits. The same can be said for dogs—not only do dogs enjoy being outside, they also enjoy being with you. Plus, studies show that dogs can sense our stress, so by taking care of your mental health, you're also helping your dog.

It takes your bond to new levels. Whether you've just adopted a puppy or have a dog that's been by your side for ten years, outdoor adventuring can lead to incredible shared experiences. One-on-one time in nature means you get to focus on each other—no screens, routines, or other distractions—so you'll understand each other more. Working together to face whatever scenarios nature puts you in also earns trust. Top all that with achieving an adventure goal or visiting a bucket-list place together, and you can begin to understand how life-changing adventuring with your dog can be for both of you.

Loki is ready for his close-up!

PHOTOGRAPHY CREDITS

OPPOSITE: Little Skipper in a big world.

ACKNOWLEDGMENTS

Camping With Dogs would like to thank Jordan Holt for the hard work she put into making this book a reality, and Brandon Watson, who was an early believer in our entrepreneurial journey.

L. J. Tracosas would like to thank Camping With Dogs for the opportunity to work on this book. Getting to know members of your warm, adventurous, and kindhearted community was a joy. Thank you to Rage Kindelsperger for the opportunity to work with your fantastic team, especially Katie McGuire, editor extraordinaire, who provided excellent and thoughtful edits, as well as next-level project management. Thanks to Silverglass Design for your beautiful work, and for polishing it all until it shines. Endless gratitude to my friend and colleague, Delia Greve, for connecting me with the project and being my adventure buddy. Thank you to my family: my dog-obsessed son, Nolan; my amazing husband, Sam, who promised me we could get a dog this summer (it's in print now!); my son Miles, who inspires me daily; and our cats, Bruce and Flerken—thank you for helping us laugh again.

Most of all, thank you to all of the contributors to this book: Every conversation I had with you all gave me goosebumps or made me cry, or (often) both—and every single one made me think about connections and a life well lived and well loved. Thank you so much for sharing your stories and your dog friends with us.

OPPOSITE: Lunatic is cool as a cucumber chilling at the crag at Kraft Boulders, Nevada.

ABOUT THE AUTHORS

Every dog has a story, and Camping With Dogs wants to share it.

What started in Nashville, Tennessee, in 2015 as an Instagram account featuring photos of dogs going on adventures in the great outdoors has become so much more. It has become a community of people who are passionate about spending quality time outside with their dogs. We receive hundreds of photos every day of members of this community who want to share their adventures with their dogs. Each photo we receive showcases the incredible bonds that have been created between dogs and their owners in the Camping With Dogs community.

We strive to create an environment to bring members of the Camping With Dogs community together. Whether that has been through the growth of our social media or connecting with dog owners on a personal level, we are thrilled to have a space where lovers of the outdoors and dogs can relate to one another. Camping With Dogs has a passion for bringing together a diverse group of hikers, campers, and dog owners. From Nashville, Tennessee to Seattle, Washington to Scotland and Australia, we are a community thousands strong with furry companions that make life so much more special.

L. J. Tracosas is a writer and editor. She's the author of more than twenty nonfiction books for curious young readers and adults. She lives in Atlanta with her husband, son, and two cats, and makes books in memory of her son Miles.

OPPOSITE PAGE: Polar bear mode! Riley and her humans went for a 10k winter hike in Blue Mountain in Ontario, Canada. She enjoyed every minute.
FOLLOWING PAGES: Lunatic takes her ball to see the beautiful sunset views over the Colorado River at Glen Canyon Dam, Arizona.

© 2023 by Quarto Publishing Group USA Inc.

First published in 2023 by Epic Ink, an imprint of The Quarto Group,
142 West 36th Street, 4th Floor, New York, NY 10018, USA
T (212) 779-4972 F (212) 779-6058 www.Quarto.com

Epic Ink titles are also available at discount for retail, wholesale, promotional, and bulk purchase. For details, contact the Special Sales Manager by email at specialsales@quarto.com or by mail at The Quarto Group, Attn: Special Sales Manager, 100 Cummings Center Suite 265D, Beverly, MA 01915 USA.

10 9 8 7 6 5 4 3 2 1

ISBN: 978-0-7603-8137-3

Library of Congress Cataloging-in-Publication Data

Names: Tracosas, L. J., author.
Title: Every dog deserves an adventure : amazing stories of camping with
   dogs / Camping with Dogs with L.J. Tracosas.
Description: New York, NY : Epic Ink, an imprint of The Quarto Group, 2023.
   | Summary: "In Every Dog Deserves an Adventure, the Camping With Dogs
   team shares stories, photos, safety tips, and hiking bucket lists to
   inspire you to get outside and enjoy nature with your dog"-- Provided by
   publisher.
Identifiers: LCCN 2023002520 (print) | LCCN 2023002521 (ebook) | ISBN
   9780760381373 (hardcover) | ISBN 9780760381380 (ebook)
Subjects: LCSH: Camping with dogs. | Camping with dogs--Anecdotes.
Classification: LCC SF427.455 .T73 2023 (print) | LCC SF427.455 (ebook) |
   DDC 796.54--dc23/eng/20230215
LC record available at https://lccn.loc.gov/2023002520

Group Publisher: Rage Kindelsperger
Creative Director: Laura Drew
Managing Editor: Cara Donaldson
Editor: Katie McGuire
Cover and Interior Design: Silverglass

Printed in China